SHEIR

SIMPLE

HEALTHY

EASY

INEXPENSIVE

RECIPES

by Marva Riley

Editors:
Karen Yvonne Hamilton, *Yesterday Press,* www.yesterdaypress.com
Shakeba Thomas Shields, *Get SET Edit*, www.getsetedit.com

Cover Design:
Susan Gulash, Creative Director/Owner, *Gulash Graphics*

DEDICATION

To my beautiful granddaughters Aria, Esti and Ambria.

Oh, the delight you bring me.

Reviews

I love this book! If you're looking for a good source of plant-based meals that's enjoyable and flavorful, look no further. Marva shares her passion to encourage others to eat better for a healthy lifestyle. Marva has put forward recipes based upon her personal journey to healing and good health. These recipes contain ingredients that are affordable and easy to find in your local grocery store or farmer's market. I've prepared and enjoyed some of these recipes and encourage you to do the same—Marie McKenzie, MBA, BA-HCS, BSN, RN, #1 Amazon Bestselling Author of *Things That Keep Me Up at Night*.

>>

SHEIR is an amazing cookbook that provides short, simple, healthy, easy, and most important for me----inexpensive recipes. With the rising cost of everything, including food, it is refreshing and a relief to have access to recipes that are not only healthy and easy to prepare but fits into my food budget. After reviewing the ingredients in all the recipes, I realize that I can get everything at my regular grocery store; I do not have to go to specialty stores and spend extra to get the necessary foods to maintain my healthy eating lifestyle.

My name is Althea L. Essue, and I am a Certified Personal Trainer and a Licensed Massage Therapist. In my line of work, I encounter individuals who are on their own journey towards health and fitness. As a Personal Trainer, I often train clients who are not just interested in improving their health through physical activity, they also want to improve their nutrition by eating low fat foods, more natural vegetables, fruits, and grains. They also express the desire to be able to prepare home cooked meals that are healthy and inexpensive. As a Licensed Massage Therapist, I encounter clients who require massage therapy to alleviate certain issues such as sore muscles, stiff joints, chronic diseases, and pain from various accidents. While massage therapy is a form of rehabilitation, some clients can benefit from a change in their nutrition/diet to assist with their healing.

SHEIR is for the beginner who is looking to change their eating habits/style, for the intermediate who is looking for a variety of healthy meals, so they do not get bored, and for the expert who wants to maintain their healthy lifestyle.

I cannot wait to make some of these dishes, especially the ones that are fast and easy. Just because I have a busy life doesn't mean that I have to eat unhealthy food. Get your copy of SHEIR today, and why not get one or twenty for your friends. They will thank you. - Althea L. Essue, BS, LMT, CPT

TABLE OF CONTENTS

A Note from Marva

Losing excess weight often results in a few gains! Your energy will increase, and your self-esteem will also get a boost.

Clearly, yo-yo dieting doesn't work! Allow me to show you how simple and easy it is to include very healthy, delicious, and easy meals in your busy schedule. A pinch of this and a dash of that, these recipes will tantalize your taste buds and nourish your body. Have some fun in the kitchen. Be a little crazy and create while eating for life.

All the exercise in the world without proper nutrition and healthy eating will get you nowhere. I am convinced that people want to lose weight. They want to feel good and look their best. They want to get off those pills. They want to eat well and stop the roller coaster yo-yo dieting. They just don't know how.

Many think it's expensive to eat healthy. Some think it'll take up too much of the little time they have to spare. Not true. Eating healthy can be quite easy if you do a little bit of planning and tap into your creativity.

Allow me to show you how.

Marva

INTRODUCTION

Or do you not know that your body is a temple of the Holy Spirit within you, whom you have from God? You are not your own, for you were bought with a price. So, glorify God in your body. 1 Corinthians 6:19-20 ESV

Healthy living begins with learning HOW to eat healthy. In this book, I will teach you the art of creative, healthy cooking. The art of healthy eating. You will learn to prepare Simple, Healthy, Easy, Inexpensive Recipes to nourish your body and please your taste buds.

Gautama Buddha says, "To keep the body in good health is a duty... otherwise we shall not be able to keep our mind strong and clear." Food heals and food kills, it's our choice. Is your health worth the effort?

We are always tweaking our diet. Our diet determines our lifespan and the quality of our lifespan. Eating well requires people to be creative with their meals. Your kitchen is your laboratory. This means that it's a place of experiment and experience. There you'll learn and have fun because life was meant to be fun.

In addition, go for a walk after you eat. Go back to the old traditions of dining with your family at the table where wonderful conversations take place, food is enjoyed, and bonding occurs.

With Love,

Marva

TIPS FOR SUCCESS

Here are a few tips to help you to lose those extra pounds and keep them off. They work for me, and I want to share them with you. I am well aware that many folks focus a lot on weight loss and become quite discouraged when the result isn't what they expect. I suggest that the focus should never be on weight loss, but rather on a healthy lifestyle, of which weight loss is a byproduct.

Here we go:

1. Plan ahead to succeed.

2. Buy a lunch bag/lunch kit and a few glass containers with lids to pack your lunch.

3. Learn to cook. There are plenty of healthy recipes online, on my website, and on my YouTube channel. Be creative with your cooking to make it tasty and flavorful.

4. Bring your lunch + snacks to work with you. It's healthier and cheaper. Stay away from that cafeteria and restaurant.

5. Eat more veggies and fruits.

6. Include a Raw Veggie Salad with lunch and dinner. Salads keep you feeling full and are low in calories yet nutrient dense.

7. Minimize or eliminate processed foods. They generally have sugar and or salt added to preserve. Eat fresh foods.

8. Minimize salt and sugar.

9. Drink an adequate amount of water. Infuse with fruits and veggies like cucumber, lime, lemon, ginger, and turmeric if you can't stand the taste of water like myself. Water helps to keep you well hydrated and feeling full.

10. If possible, have nothing to eat after 7pm (check with your medical provider if you have health issues like diabetes). Just before 7pm, grab a snack with 1 apple and a handful of nuts.

11. Eat your heaviest meal for lunch.

12. Eat apples and berries or a few nuts; these are healthy between meals snacks that are low in calories.

13. Walk for 30 minutes at least 4 days per week.

14. Cook and parcel your lunch in containers, enough for a few days.

15. Grab a container in the mornings. Throw in fruits, nuts and water. You'll be prepared for the day and less likely to buy that junk in the snack machine at work.

16. Get adequate sleep! Insufficient sleep can lead to weight gain and weight retention.

17. Go easy on the carbs. 1 potato is better than 2. 1 spoon of rice is better than 2.

RECIPES

Dear Readers,

    SHEIR is an atypical Recipe Book and is not necessarily written with specific measurements as most recipe and cookbooks are. I wrote this book to encourage you to be a creative alchemist in your own kitchen. Feel free to add "a pinch of this and a dash of that" to your favorite spices to create delightful, tasty, and healthy meals for you and your family.

"Let thy food be thy medicine, and let thy medicine be thy food."

Greek physician Hippocrates

FOUNDATION SPICES

You think you like meat. But you don't. It's the spices and the condiments that you like.

Put spices and condiments like peppers, onion, garlic, tomato, cumin, coriander, curry, turmeric powder, fennel, ginger, caraway, Jamaican jerk seasoning, seasoning salt, sea salt, thyme, ginger, and black pepper in your vegetables and you'll think that you're eating meat.

TIP: The key to enjoying veggies is to spice it up; nice it up. Don't be afraid of mixing any spice to your raw or cooked veggies, beans, peas, or grains.

Eating to live means that we learn to enjoy the natural flavors of plant-based foods. Some of the most nutrient rich foods are not sweet, they are actually bitter or tart. Try to stay away from processed spices. Use real onion and real garlic instead of garlic or onion powder. Anything processed has additives which are not always disclosed on the labels.

Marva's Favorite Spices and Seasonings

Although I do enjoy cooking, I am also what I call *Lazy in the Kitchen.* Hence, my foods, though tasty, are prepared in a simple fashion. Adding a pinch of this, and a dash of that, you too can create your own special, tasty, delicious, easy, inexpensive, and nutrient rich meals every day.

These spices and seasonings add flavor to any food, making them tasty, delicious, and healthy. These are natural and healthy flavors. For example, did you know that mint can be added to fruit salads and vegetable salads?

Whether cooking meat or vegetables, these spices and seasonings will add a zesty flavor that will cause your mouth to water. They're healthy and have healing properties.

Allspice
Avocado & seed oil
Bell peppers of every color
Black pepper
Caraway seeds
Clove
Coconut oil and milk
Coriander
Cumin
Fennel seeds
Garlic cloves (fresh)
Ginger root
Green Onion/Scallion
Jamaican curry powder
Jamaican jerk sauce

Nuts of all kinds
Mints of all varieties
Onion (not powder)
Paprika
Pimento/allspice (whole or powder)
Red peppers (crushed)
Ripe tomato
Rosemary leaves
Sea salt
Spicy peppers like scotch bonnet
Sweet peppers
Turmeric root
Thyme

So, why use these spices?

Turmeric contains Curcumin, a substance with powerful anti-inflammatory effects. Its cousin Ginger can be used fresh, dried, or powdered and may be helpful for digestion, nausea and vomiting, and inflammation. Ginger may also help to boost the immune system and ward off infections.

Cayenne, for example, contains capsaicin which may help to reduce appetite and may have anti-cancer properties. Cayenne has been referred to as the red dynamite. It contains a phytochemical called capsaicin which helps to promote blood flow to tissues by lowering blood pressure and by stimulating the release of nitric oxide that helps to expand blood vessels. Research indicates that eating cayenne pepper may be beneficial in increasing circulation, improving the strength of blood vessels and it may reduce the build-up of plaques in the arteries. Cayenne contains capsaicin which may help to reduce appetite and may have anti-cancer properties.

Garlic dates back to almost 6,000 years and was often prescribed as a digestive purge, for internal and external infections. This includes inflammation such as cough and respiratory infections and is also a general tonic for the body.

Onion helps to improve circulation by helping the arteries and veins to widen when blood flow increases. Onions are rich in the antioxidant flavonoid which benefits heart health and improves circulation. Onion also has anti-inflammatory properties.

Fennel and **Caraway** are used for digestive problems including heartburn, bloating, gas, loss of appetite, and spasms of the stomach and intestines. Caraway is also beneficial for sleep and relaxation due to its magnesium content. They're also rich in potassium, calcium, iron, protein, and other minerals.

Pimento or **Allspice** has eugenol which helps to relieve diarrhea, nausea, vomiting, and even constipation. The antioxidants present in pimento also have anti-inflammatory qualities that may reduce cramps and aid digestion. Pimento also has anesthetic and analgesic properties that help to relieve pain and relax muscles.

Now let's cook our
way to health...

SAUCES

Homemade Cranberry Sauce without Sugar

Cranberries are naturally tart. Nutritional benefits include antioxidants that support the immune system and help to prevent urinary tract infection. Canned cranberries are not as tart as this homemade sauce as they're heavily sweetened with sugar which is bad for our health.

INGREDIENTS

1 pound cranberries

1 cup honey

½ cup water

1 cup freshly squeezed orange juice

½ tsp cinnamon (optional)

DIRECTIONS

Wash cranberries. Bring water to boil on medium heat. Add cranberries and stir. Reduce heat to low.

Stir in honey, orange juice and cinnamon. Cook for about 15 minutes until the sauce thickens. When cool, you can keep it in the refrigerator for up to two weeks. May eat warm or cool.

>>>

Nigerian Red Sauce

Can be served with meats, fish, stew or any cooked vegetable dish.

INGREDIENTS

6 ripe red tomatoes

1 large red bell pepper

1 large onion

4 cloves garlic

3 slices ginger root

¼ cup olive oil

2 tablespoon Maggi Chicken Noodle Soup Mix

DIRECTIONS

Blend tomatoes, cook in a pot to dry out the water. This becomes a paste like canned tomato paste. Blend bell pepper, onion, garlic, and ginger. Set aside. In a pot, add tomato paste and olive oil. Cook over low heat, stirring frequently for about 10 minutes. Add other ingredients. Stir frequently. Add a pinch of salt as needed to taste.

BEVERAGES

Oftentimes, we experience fatigue, headaches, and difficulty focusing. Irregular heartbeat, low or high blood pressure, rapid heart rate, indigestion, constipation, urinary tract infections, dry skin, skin aging, and even low immunity can also occur as a result of underhydration.

Here are a few health benefits of drinking plenty of water: Helps to normalize your blood pressure and stabilize your heart rate. Improves sleep and mood. Adds more energy. Builds healthy joints and muscles. Carries oxygen and nutrients to your blood cells. Flushes toxins from the body. Aids in digestion. Prevents constipation. Keeps the skin young and clear.

TIP: Never use processed sugar as it is inflammatory and will derail your health journey. Inflammatory conditions like diabetes, sinusitis, and cancer thrive on sugar.

Drinking Water (Veggie or Fruit Infused)

6 to 8 glasses of water is the recommended amount and will help you to feel more energetic and clearer minded.

INGREDIENTS	DIRECTIONS
Pineapple Ginger root Cucumber Strawberries Lime/lemon juice	It's also fun to do combos like ginger and pineapples or strawberries and mint. Add your desired quantity to drinking water to make it interesting and tasty.

>>>

Pumpkin Drink

Drink at room temperature or with ice.

INGREDIENTS	DIRECTIONS
Yellow pumpkin squash A pinch of cinnamon powder ¼ teaspoon real vanilla A pinch of nutmeg I cup coconut milk	Wash and cook pumpkin with the skin on and boil. Add a pinch of salt. Cool and puree. Then add a cup of coconut milk, cinnamon, vanilla and nutmeg.

>>

Cucumber Drink

Place everything in your blender/juicer and blend until liquified.

Cucumber Celery Apples	Spinach Coconut water

Jamaican Style Pineapple Drink

Best when served chilled. You may add a bit of your favorite alcohol as desired for a nice kick.

INGREDIENTS

Skin of 1 properly washed
& peeled pineapple
Ginger root mashed
1 thin slice turmeric root
mashed
3 whole pimentos

DIRECTIONS

Wash outside of pineapple to remove all dirt/residue. Peel the pineapple. Add the skins only to a large pot of water. Peel several fingers of ginger root, and gently beat/mash the ginger to open up the root.

Bring pineapple skins, whole pimento, ginger roots and turmeric to a boil, then turn off the heat. Allow to steep for a few hours until cool, then strain.

Sweeten with honey to taste (optional). Transfer contents from pot to a large pitcher. Store the juice in the refrigerator.

>>

Immune Booster Tea

Sweeten with raw organic unfiltered honey (optional).

INGREDIENTS

2 cups water
¼ lemon or lime in skin
1 inch ginger root mashed
1 teaspoon turmeric
powder
½ apple

DIRECTIONS

Add all ingredients to water.

Boil on low heat for 20 minutes.

Remove from heat. Strain and enjoy.

Moringa & Dandelion Tea

This tea can help with sleep and relaxation at night. It has many great nutrients, such as magnesium, protein, vitamin C, iron and vitamin A, to help nourish our bodies. Save extra in the refrigerator and reheat when ready to drink.

INGREDIENTS

32 ounces water
1 handful moringa leaves with stems
4 dried soursop leaves
½ handful dried dandelion leaves

OPTIONAL: raw, organic honey.

DIRECTIONS

Bring water to boil. Lower heat to simmer.

Add all the ingredients. Simmer for 10 minutes. Turn off heat. Let brew for 10 minutes.

Strain. Store extra tea in the refrigerator and reheat as needed.

OPTIONAL: add a tad of raw, organic honey.

>>

Sleep & Relaxation Tea

INGREDIENTS

2 dried or green soursop leaves
1 handful of dried moringa leaves
Mint of choice
Mashed or grated ginger root
4 cups water

DIRECTIONS

Bring water to boil. Add all ingredients.

Reduce heat to low. Boil for 20 minutes.

OPTIONAL: Sweeten with a bit of raw organic unfiltered honey.

Tea for Inflammation

INGREDIENTS

Turmeric root (mashed or
grated)
1 tablespoon dandelion root
12 ounces water

DIRECTIONS

Bring water to boil.
Add both roots. Boil for 20
minutes. Strain and enjoy.

>>>

Digestive Herbal Tea

This tea is excellent for flatus/excess gas, heartburn, and bloating. The ingredients have anti-inflammatory properties, antioxidants, and may help to treat or prevent cancer and heart disease. It is an excellent pain reliever and helps with sleep.

INGREDIENTS

Fresh organic ginger root
(mashed or grated)
Fresh organic turmeric
root (mashed or grated)
1 teaspoon fennel seeds
and/or caraway seeds
Mint of choice
20 ounces water

DIRECTIONS

Bring water to boil in a pot. Add the ingredients. Turn heat down and boil on low for 20 minutes.

Turn off heat and let brew for 2 hours.

Sweeten with raw organic honey to taste (optional).

TIP: Make enough to last for about three days, reheating just the needed amount each time.

Ginger & Turmeric Herbal tea

Beneficial with seasonal allergies, sinus congestion and headaches, nausea, bloating and gas, joint and muscle pains. Reduces inflammation and strengthens the immune system.

INGREDIENTS

Ginger
Turmeric
Pinch of Cayenne powder
Fresh lime or lemon juice

DIRECTIONS

Blend ginger and turmeric. Add to a cup of hot water. Mix in the cayenne and lime or lemon juice. Add a bit of honey if desired.

>>>

Mango & Mixed Fruit Smoothie

Blend everything together and enjoy.

INGREDIENTS

Mango
Strawberries
Raspberries
Blackberries

Bananas

1/2 cup orange juice and 1/2 cup almond milk

>>>

Mixed Fruit Smoothie

Blend everything together and enjoy.

INGREDIENTS

½ handful pecan nuts
1 teaspoon dandelion leaf powder
4 strawberries
½ green apple

½ ripe banana
¼ teaspoon chia seeds
¼ teaspoon whole flax seeds
¼ teaspoon hemp seeds
1 slice ginger root

Apple, Banana, Strawberry Smoothie

Blend everything together and enjoy.

INGREDIENTS

½ green apple
½ banana
4 strawberries
1 slice ginger root

1 teaspoon dandelion powder
½ handful unsalted pecan nuts
A few moringa leaves

BREAKFAST

*Food is medicine! Breaking your fast...When you choose the right foods you are setting yourself up **for a great day. Food is Medicine.***

Oatmeal with Oat Milk

Stir together in a bowl.

INGREDIENTS

Steel Cut oatmeal
Oat milk
Flaxseed
Chia seed

Cinnamon
Grated nutmeg
Almond butter
½ banana for sweetness
May heat oat milk or eat
cold as desired

>>>

Old Fashioned Oatmeal

INGREDIENTS

Flax
Chia
Hemp seeds
1 cup old fashioned oatmeal
2 cups water

OPTIONAL: coconut oil or
coconut milk may be added.

DIRECTIONS

Bring water to boil.
Add the oatmeal, flax, chia and
hemp seeds.
Reduce heat to low

Cook for 5 minutes.

Top with strawberries,
blueberries, cinnamon, nutmeg,
vanilla.

DESSERTS & SNACKS

Everyone enjoys a delicious dessert or snack, but oftentimes we reach for a sugar laden cookie, cake, ice cream, donuts etc. How about something a bit healthier that will taste great but won't add 5 inches and 10 pounds to the hips, butts and thighs?

Cauliflower - Buffalo Bites

INGREDIENTS

Cauliflower
5 ounces hot sauce
Vegan Ranch Dressing

DIRECTIONS

Chop up cauliflower and put in a bowl. Wash and pat dry. Then pour a bottle of hot sauce in the bowl. Shake well and let sit for at least 24 hours in the fridge.

You may prefer to put jalapeño pepper on them, or you can serve them plain. Put in the air fryer for 20 minutes and enjoy it with your favorite vegan ranch dressing.

>>

Brain Food Mix Dessert

Mix everything together and enjoy.

INGREDIENTS

Dandelion powder (optional)
Organic raw honey
Organic coconut oil
Pecan nuts
Pinch cayenne powder

Organic cocoa bits
Grapes, pineapple (fruit of choice)
Dairy free yogurt

Curried Jackfruit Seeds

INGREDIENTS

¼ cup coconut milk
4 tablespoons curry powder
1 tablespoon coriander
powder
¼ teaspoon cumin powder
¼ teaspoon cinnamon
powder
1 tablespoon turmeric
powder
¼ cup olive oil
2 to 3 cups jackfruit seeds
1 chopped onion
4 finely chopped garlic cloves
Pinch clove powder
1 tomato chopped small
Salt to taste
Pinch crushed red pepper

DIRECTIONS

Remove the outer film from jackfruit seeds and cook till soft. Mash cooked jackfruit seeds in a mortar.

In a large wok, heat oil on medium heat. Add curry, turmeric powder, cumin, cinnamon, and clove powder. Stir.

Add onion, garlic, and tomato. Stir. Add coconut milk. Reduce heat to low. Stir. Add jackfruit. Stir well.

Add remaining ingredients. Cook on low heat for about 15 minutes.

Serve with rice, quinoa, salad, or any grain.

>>>

Almond Butter Dessert

INGREDIENTS

1 tbsp almond butter
Raw organic unfiltered honey
Fuji apple cut in small pieces

DIRECTIONS

Pour honey over almond butter. Dip the apple in and enjoy. Serve with a cup of hot organic unsweetened cacao beverage.

Cacao Dessert

INGREDIENTS

1 tablespoon raw 100% cacao powder
¼ teaspoon raw organic blackstrap molasses
¼ teaspoon coconut oil
Almond or favorite nut pieces
A few pieces of favorite fruit

DIRECTIONS

Mix everything together. Place in the freezer. Remove when hardened.

>>

Cacao, Peanut Butter, Banana Dessert

INGREDIENTS

Mashed ripe banana
1 teaspoon raw organic cacao powder
Peanut butter

DIRECTIONS

Mix everything together.

Enjoy.

>>

Oatmeal Cookies Dessert

INGREDIENTS

2 ripe bananas mashed
2 ½ cups of oatmeal
1 tablespoon maple syrup
2 eggs or egg substitute whipped
1 handful of Raisins

DIRECTIONS

Mix ingredients together.

Bake for 12 minutes at 350.

Super Bowl Lentil Dip

INGREDIENTS

Cooked lentils (substitute for ground beef)
Dairy free cream cheese
Salsa medium
Almond cheese
Tomatoes
Taco seasoning

DIRECTIONS

Brown lentils and season with taco seasoning. In the bottom of a pan, spread dairy free cream cheese, then spread lentils, slice a tomato on top of lentils and then spread salsa over tomatoes and top with almond cheese. Place in the oven on 350 for 20 minutes.

>>>

Sweet Potato Dessert

INGREDIENTS

Sweet potatoes
Honey
Cinnamon
Nutmeg

DIRECTIONS

Cook sweet potatoes until tender. Mash. Add honey, cinnamon, and nutmeg. Mix. Can substitute sweet potatoes for pumpkin.

>>>

Fruits & Spinach Mix Dessert

Mix everything and enjoy.

INGREDIENTS

Dairy free yogurt (from coconut)
Honey
Lime juice
2 cups spinach cut tiny

Lettuce shredded
Grapefruit sectioned
Seedless purple grapes

Trini Doubles: Trinidadian Fried Dough with Curried Chickpeas

Dough INGREDIENTS

½ cup warm water
¼ teaspoon honey
1 teaspoon yeast
2 cups all-purpose flour
½ teaspoon salt
1 teaspoon ground turmeric
½ teaspoon ground cumin
½ teaspoon ground black pepper

Dough DIRECTIONS

Place the warm water, honey, and yeast in a separate small bowl. Set aside until the mixture bubbles.

In a large bowl combine the flour, salt, turmeric, cumin, and black pepper. Stir the yeast mixture into the flour mixture and add additional lukewarm water as needed—about ½ cup until the mixture comes together into slightly firm dough. Knead until smooth and elastic and cover with a damp cloth.

Set aside in a warm place to rise until doubled in size, about an hour.

Filling INGREDIENTS

1 pound cooked chickpeas (garbanzo beans)
1 tablespoon olive oil
1 onion, thinly sliced
3 garlic cloves, minced
4 ½ teaspoons curry powder
1 pinch ground cumin
Salt & freshly ground black pepper
Olive Oil (for frying)
Hot pepper sauce, for serving
Finely shredded cucumber, for garnish

Filling DIRECTIONS

It is best to use freshly cooked chickpeas. Canned chickpeas have quite a bit of added sodium. If using canned chickpeas, drain and rinse well with cold water.

Heat the oil on medium in a large pot and add the onion. Cook until golden. Add the garlic and stir well, frying for 1 minute more. Add the curry powder and mix well. Cook for 30 seconds and add ¼ cup of water.

Stir in the chickpeas, cover and simmer for 5 minutes. Remove the lid and add 1 more cup of water.

Stir in the cumin, and salt and
pepper, and lower the heat.
Simmer until the chickpeas are very
tender.

To complete the doubles: Punch down the dough and allow it to sit for 10 minutes. Pinch off walnut-size pieces of dough and flatten each into a circle about 4 1/2 inches in diameter. Dampen your hands with water if the dough is sticky.

Heat about 1 cup of olive oil, at least 3 inches deep in a frying pan or medium saucepan. Test the oil by sprinkling a bit of flour into it. If the flour bubbles and sizzles, the oil is ready.

Add the dough circles and fry, turning once, until lightly browned on both sides, about 40 seconds. Place 2 tablespoons of chickpeas on each piece of fried dough. Add the pepper sauce, Kuchela*, and cucumber, if desired. Top with another piece of fried dough. Serve.

Kuchela is a spicy condiment made from green mangoes and Scotch bonnet peppers, which can be found in Caribbean stores.

>>

Jackfruit Seed Hummus

INGREDIENTS	DIRECTIONS
2 cups jackfruit seeds	Boil seeds with a pinch of salt. Until tender Strip off film. Place in a bullet blender.
1/4 tsp salt	
½ tsp chopped ginger root	
1 tablespoon honey	Add ginger, honey, yellow mustard, vegetable broth and olive oil.
Yellow mustard 1 tablespoon	
¼ cup olive oil	Blend until smooth.
¼ cup vegetable broth	

Chocolate Bar Dessert

INGREDIENTS

Chocolate bar 90% cacao
Almond nut butter or peanut butter

DIRECTIONS

Simply top the chocolate bar with nut butter and enjoy.

>>

Papa's Healthy Fudgy Wudgy

Enjoy this finger lickin healthy dessert.

INGREDIENTS

100% organic cacao powder
Coconut oil
Dandelion root and flower
powder (optional)
Chia seeds
Walnuts
Raw Organic unfiltered honey
Banana or favorite fruit
A bit of water

DIRECTIONS

Mix everything and pour into a plastic container.

Sprinkle it with cayenne pepper powder.

Place in the freezer. Remove when frozen.

>>

Fried Sweet Plantains

INGREDIENTS

Very ripe plantain that is soft and almost black (the riper the plantain, the sweeter)

Olive oil or oil of choice.

DIRECTIONS

Cut into long strips not too thin, not too thick. Heat oil until it's very hot. Lower plantain in oil (being careful not to splash). *Do not leave unattended as ripe plantain burns very quickly.*

Flip plantain when golden brown. Remove when both sides are a nice golden brown. Place on a paper towel to absorb excess oil.

BEANS & PEAS

Red beans. Black beans. Kidney beans. Lentils. Chickpeas. All are healthy. All beans are quite nutritious and are great alternatives to meat, fish, seafood and animal-based foods.

Nutrients in beans and peas include protein, iron, carbohydrates, fiber, calcium, potassium, and some healthy fats. As you can see, there are ample plant based protein, iron, calcium and fats; therefore, there should not be any concerns as to whether we can get adequate amounts of these nutrients eating a predominantly plant based diet as opposed to meats and dairy products.

Aim to eat freshly cooked foods and try your best to avoid canned, frozen and processed foods which usually contain too much salt or other unhealthy preservatives which are sometimes not even listed on the label.

Cooking Beans from Scratch

Cook your beans from scratch. Canned beans have preservatives and additives, and the food industry is not required to put all its additives on the label. Many processed foods, including canned foods have added salt, sugar, unhealthy preservatives and even some food colorings which are known potential carcinogens.

For dry, hard beans like chickpeas, black and red bean:

The juice can be used to cook rice or soup, drink as a broth, and even used to sauté or gently cook veggies. Add cooked beans to salads. Curry or sautéed beans with your favorite veggies or by itself with your favorite spices and seasonings or just eat them by themselves.

INGREDIENTS

1 pound hard beans
¼ onion chopped
2 cloves garlic minced
4 whole cloves
4 whole pimento/allspice
Salt to taste
Pinch crushed red pepper
Fresh or dried thyme
¼ tsp fennel seeds
2 slices ginger root minced

DIRECTIONS

Wash beans twice and drain. Remove any debris. In a deep pot, add about 6 cups of water.

Place in the refrigerator overnight to soak or add hot water and soak for 4 hours.

Pour off water. Add about 6 cups of hot water. Add all the ingredients. Cook until tender. Place extra in the refrigerator for use later.

Beans and Peas are much cheaper than meats and are filling and quite nutritious.

Black Beans & Cabbage

INGREDIENTS

Salad:
Bok choy finely cut
Italian Parsley finely cut
2 slices onion minced
Handful walnuts
½ raw sweet potato grated
2 tablespoons apple cider vinegar

Meat Substitute: Cooked black beans
Shredded cabbage
½ green bell pepper chopped
1 small onion chopped small
3 cloves garlic minced
2 ripe tomatoes chopped
2 slices ginger root minced
2 tablespoons coconut oil

DIRECTIONS

Salad: Mix ingredients. Sprinkle 1 teaspoon chia seeds on top.

Meat Substitute: Heat oil on low. Add all meat substitute ingredients. Add salt, crushed red pepper, and allspice to your liking. Stir well. Sauté for about 15 minutes.

Served with baked sweet potato.

>>>

Curried Black Beans

Heat coconut oil on low. Stir in all ingredients. Cover and simmer for 5 minutes.

INGREDIENTS

Cooked black beans
Red onion, chopped
4 cloves fresh garlic
Fresh or dried thyme
Pinch of allspice powder
Pinch fennel seeds
1 ripe tomato chopped

Sautéed String Beans with Lentils

INGREDIENTS

1 pound string beans washed and cut into 1 inch strips
1 small onion chopped
4 cloves fresh garlic chopped
1 slice ginger roots minced
1 medium ripe tomato chopped
½ teaspoon powdered allspice
¼ red bell pepper chopped
1 teaspoon crushed red pepper
¼ teaspoon sea salt
⅛ cup olive oil (or less)
1 cup cooked and drained lentils
1 slice turmeric root minced

DIRECTIONS

Remove stems of beans. Cook until tender. Drain.

Heat oil on medium heat. Add garlic. Fry garlic until golden. Add onion, tomato, ginger root, bell pepper, turmeric root, lentils. Stir well.

Add salt, red pepper, and allspice. Stir well. Reduce heat to low.

Stir in string beans. Reduce heat to simmer. Let simmer for 15 minutes. Serve over Rice or Quinoa

>>>

Spicy Sautéed String Beans

INGREDIENTS

1 pound string beans
1 small onion chopped
4 cloves fresh garlic chopped
1 slice ginger roots minced
1 medium ripe tomato chopped
½ teaspoon powdered allspice
¼ red bell pepper chopped
1 teaspoon crushed red pepper
¼ teaspoon sea salt
⅛ cup olive oil (or less)

DIRECTIONS

Wash green beans, remove stems, cut into 1 inch strips. Remove stems. Cook until tender. Drain.

Heat oil on medium heat. Add garlic. Fry garlic until golden. Add onion, tomato, ginger root, bell pepper. Stir well.

Add salt, red pepper, and allspice. Stir well. Stir in string beans. Reduce heat to simmer. Let simmer for 15 minutes. Serve over Rice or Quinoa

Curried Green Beans

INGREDIENTS

1 pound green beans
1 large onion chopped into
tiny bits
4 cloves fresh garlic cut small
¼ small tomato cut small
1 slice ginger root minced
½ green sweet pepper cut
small
¼ cup coconut milk
2 tablespoons spicy Jamaican
curry powder
1 teaspoon spicy Jamaican jerk
sauce
¼ cup olive oil
¼ teaspoon salt
Pinch of allspice

DIRECTIONS

Wash green beans, remove stems, cut into strips about ¼ inch.

Boil green beans. Drain. Save ¼ cup of the water. In a large pot, add oil. Heat. Add curry to oil and stir.

Mix in jerk sauce and coconut milk. Add all other ingredients except beans. Stir and lower heat to low setting.

Stir. Add beans. Stir well. Cover and let simmer for about 15 minutes.

If there isn't enough juice, add a bit of the juice from the cooked beans.

String Beans & Mushrooms

INGREDIENTS

1 pound string beans washed
and cut into small pieces
Mushrooms washed and each
cut into pieces
1 large onion chopped small
3 cloves fresh garlic cut into
small pieces
1 large ripe tomato cut small
1 red sweet pepper cut into
small pieces
¼ teaspoon crushed red
peppers
Salt to taste
Pinch of black pepper
Pinch of allspice
Cooking oil of choice

DIRECTIONS

Cook and drain string beans. Pour
cooking oil into the pot. Heat on
medium.

Add vegetables except beans and
mushrooms. Gently sauté.

Stir in salt, black pepper and allspice.
Mix in string beans and mushrooms.

Cover and let simmer on low for
about 15 minutes.

Serve over any grain or root
vegetable.

Chickpeas Cooked from Scratch

Chickpea broth is very delicious and is healthy.
* These ingredients need to be prepared fresh just before you're ready to cook your chickpeas.

INGREDIENTS

1 bag dried chickpeas
1/2 onion chopped
1 clove fresh garlic minced
6 whole pimentos
Pinch of salt to taste
Fresh thyme
3 whole clove buds

DIRECTIONS

Wash chickpeas twice with cold water. Drain. In a large pot, add chickpeas & fill with water until about 3 inches above the level of the chickpeas. Place in the refrigerator and leave overnight to soak.

Next day, drain and add fresh water. Add the other ingredients. Cook in a pressure cooker, slow cooker or regular pot until tender. Drain. Save the broth for soup or to be used as liquid for your other recipes.

String Beans & Cauliflower Curry

String beans and cauliflower are very nutritious, filling and very low in calories.

INGREDIENTS

2 cups string beans washed, cut into 1 inch size, cooked and drained
2 cups cauliflower steamed, cut small and drained
1 small onion chopped small
4 cloves minced garlic cloves
1 large ripe tomato
1 slice ginger root minced
1 tablespoon Jamaican spicy curry
¼ teaspoon Jamaican hot jerk sauce
Pinch allspice powder
1 tablespoon butter
1 tablespoon coconut oil
1 tablespoon olive oil
Pinch salt

DIRECTIONS

Heat butter and oils on low. Stir in curry powder, jerk sauce, allspice, and salt. Add onion, garlic, tomato, ginger. Stir well. Reduce heat to simmer.

Add string beans and cauliflower. Stir well.

Cover and let simmer for 15 minutes.

Beans & Turmeric

INGREDIENTS

1 pound green/string beans.

1 ripe tomato chopped

1 small onion chopped small

2 cloves fresh garlic minced

2 slices fresh garlic root minced finely

¼ teaspoon spicy Jamaican jerk sauce

2 tablespoons turmeric powder

¼ teaspoon salt

⅛ cup olive or coconut oil

DIRECTIONS

Remove stems from beans. Wash, drain, cut into ½ inch strips. Cook beans with salt until tender. Drain. Save ¼ cup of the water. Heat oil on medium. Mix in turmeric powder, jerk sauce. Add everything else except beans. Stir. Reduce heat to simmer.

Add beans and the saved water. Mix well. Cover and let simmer for about 15 minutes.

Serve with rice.

>>

Akara (Nigerian Dish)

INGREDIENTS

1 lb Olotu beans (brown beans)

4 red scotch bonnet peppers

2 cloves of garlic

1 medium onion chopped

2 maggie cubes

½ teaspoon salt

DIRECTIONS

Soak beans in water for 30 mins. Use your hands to squeeze beans to remove the skins. Once 80% of the skins are removed, throw away the skin and put beans in a saucepan.

Add red scotch bonnet peppers, cloves of garlic, onion, maggie cube, and salt. Add mix to the blender and add enough water to cover the beans. Blend until smooth.

Add a lot of vegetable oil to a large frying pan. Use a large spoon to scoop out beans one by one and add to the frying pan. Fry on each side until golden brown. When cooked, lay on a paper towel.

Moi moi Nigerian Vegetable dish

INGREDIENTS

1 ½ cups black eyed peas cooked, skinned, outer layer removed
1 large red bell pepper
2 spicy peppers
½ cup palm oil
1 small onion
4 teaspoons vegetable bouillon
Salt to taste
½ cup hot water

DIRECTIONS

Blend beans, bell pepper, spicy pepper, onion, and bouillon. Add ½ cup water. Blend.

Heat palm oil until it's melted. In a large bowl, mix the beans from the blender with the heated palm oil.

Fold squares with aluminum foil. Scoop beans onto each piece of foil (optional: add slices of boiled egg or cooked fish). Fold the foils tightly to close them up.

In a large pot, add 2 cups of water and bring to a boil, stack all the moi inside the pot, cover the pot and cook on medium heat for 30-45 mins.

LENTILS

There is no need to buy pre-cooked lentils. Cook your own and use them in salads, stews and soups.

Versatile Lentils

INGREDIENTS

1 pound cooked and drained lentils, (refrigerate unused portion)
4 cloves fresh garlic cut up
1 medium onion chopped
Fresh or dried rosemary leaves and stem
1 slice ginger root minced
Pinch crushed red pepper
Salt to taste
Fresh thyme

DIRECTIONS

Wash and remove debris from lentils. In a large pot, add and bring water to boil. Add enough water to cover the lentils about 1 inch above.

Add all ingredients and cook on medium heat until tender for about 20 minutes or less.

Drain when cooled.

>>

Turmeric with Lentils & Mushrooms

INGREDIENTS

1 pack organic whole mushrooms washed and halved
2 cups cooked lentils
2 tablespoons turmeric powder
¼ teaspoon crushed red pepper
Pinch of salt to taste
1 medium onion chopped
4 cloves fresh garlic minced
1 medium ripe tomato chopped
¼ red sweet pepper chopped
¼ cup olive oil

DIRECTIONS

Heat oil on low. Add turmeric powder, salt, crushed red pepper. Stir. Add onion, garlic, tomato, and mix well. Add lentils, mushrooms and stir well.

Cook for 10 minutes.

Serve with salad, roasted sweet potato or roasted Irish potato.

Lentils Dish from Scratch

Add lentils to salad. Serve over cooked rice or quinoa or eat by itself. Save the rest in the refrigerator to eat as a snack.

INGREDIENTS

1 pound dried lentils

1 medium onion chopped

3 cloves garlic chopped

1 small tomato chopped

10 whole pimento

6 whole cloves

1 teaspoon fennel seeds

½ teaspoon crushed red peppers

1 tablespoon seasoned salt

½ teaspoon chopped ginger root

1 tablespoon dried rosemary or thyme

DIRECTIONS

Wash lentils and drain water. Place lentils in a pot. Add water and other ingredients.

Let soak for 1 to 2 hours then cook for about 30 minutes until tender. Do not overcook.

Once cooked, drain and save liquids into a bowl.

>>

Curried Lentils with Coconut Milk

INGREDIENTS

2 cups lentils cooked and drained

1 small onion chopped

1 small ripe tomato chopped

2 cloves fresh garlic minced

2 tablespoons olive oil

2 tablespoons spicy Jamaican curry

⅛ teaspoon hot Jamaican jerk sauce

Pinch of allspice powder

¼ cup unsweetened coconut milk

pinch of fennel seeds

1 slice ginger root minced

DIRECTIONS

Heat oil on low. Add garlic and fry until slightly golden. Add onion, tomato, ginger, fennel seeds, curry, and allspice. Stir well.

Reduce heat to simmer. Add coconut milk and jerk sauce. Stir well. Add lentils. Stir well.

Simmer for 5 minutes. If you prefer your lentils a bit dry, let simmer a little longer until the juice is dried out.

Curried Lentils

You may omit curry for a different taste and flavor, and you may substitute lentils for cooked chickpeas.

INGREDIENTS

1 pound uncooked lentil
¼ cup cooking oil of your choice
1 stick butter (optional)
1 large carrot sliced lengthwise
1 medium sweet potato chopped
2 slices pumpkin chopped small
½ green, yellow and red peppers chopped
1 scotch bonnet or spicy pepper (red) cut finely
1 green scotch bonnet pepper whole

1 large ripe tomato chopped
1 medium onion chopped
2 large cloves garlic chopped
2 slices ginger root cut tiny pieces
½ teaspoon powdered allspice
¼ teaspoon fennel seeds
¼ teaspoon caraway seeds
¼ cup coconut milk
3 tablespoons curry powder
Seasoning salt to taste
Black pepper to taste
½ teaspoon powdered cumin
1 tablespoon dried or green thyme leaves

DIRECTIONS

Wash and drain lentils. Place in a pot with water, bring to boil then turn off heat. Let sit until cool. Strain off water. Set aside lentils. Place the pot or frying pan on the stove with medium heat. Add oil and butter. When butter is melted and oil is hot, add curry powder stirring for 2 minutes.

Stir in all chopped vegetables and spices except whole pepper. Add coconut milk. Stir. Simmer for about 10 minutes on low heat. Stir in lentils. Toss in green scotch bonnet pepper. Cover and simmer until carrots and pumpkin are tender.

Serve with rice, quinoa, and salad.

Sautéed Lentils

Delicious, easy and healthy. Beans can be cooked and sautéed with any spice we desire. Use chickpeas, black beans, red beans and lentils as well to change things up.

INGREDIENTS

1 pound dried lentils
1 medium onion
1 medium tomato
4 cloves fresh garlic
Coconut or olive oil
Salt to taste
¼ teaspoon rosemary leaves
¼ teaspoon fennel seeds
Fresh or dried mint
Pinch of crushed red pepper to taste

DIRECTIONS

Wash lentils. Remove any rocks or debris. Cook until tender, not mushy. Strain and discard water.

In a saucepan, add oil of your choice. Bring to heat. Add the onion, garlic, tomato and rosemary/thyme/mint. Stir.

Add crushed red pepper, salt to taste and fennel seeds. Sauté on low heat for about 5 minutes. Stir in the lentils. Cover and simmer for another 5 minutes.

Serve with a salad, steamed vegetables and rice.

Lentils with Broccoli florets

INGREDIENTS

3 cups cooked and drained lentils
1 small onion chopped
2 cloves garlic chopped
1 small ripe tomato chopped
1 cup broccoli florets washed
¼ teaspoon caraway seeds
¼ teaspoon allspice powder
¼ teaspoon spicy Jamaican jerk sauce
2 tablespoons olive oil
2 tablespoons coconut oil

DIRECTIONS

Heat oils in a large skillet on low heat. Add caraway seeds. Add garlic and fry until golden. Stir in onion and tomato.

Add allspice, jerk sauce, salt (optional). Mix well.

Reduce heat to simmer. Stir in lentils, mix well. Add broccoli florets. Mix. Cover and simmer for 3 minutes. Remove heat. Serve over rice.

POTATOES

Carbohydrates are macronutrients which provide the body with energy.

Ripe plantain and sweet potatoes are very nutritious and can be eaten as a main course or dessert. For dessert, sprinkle a bit of honey, cinnamon and nutmeg. Add some fruits and you've got yourself a healthy, delicious, tasty dessert without the guilt.

These brightly colored foods are rich in vitamin A which is necessary for good vision, healthy immune system, bone strength and reproduction. Sweet potatoes and plantains are also good fiber which contributes to a healthy colon.

Mixed Mashed Potatoes

INGREDIENTS

2 large sweet potatoes
4 redskin or white skin potatoes
2 tablespoons coconut oil
½ teaspoon cinnamon powder
½ teaspoon grated nutmeg
Salt to taste

DIRECTIONS

Wash potatoes well. Leave skin on. Cut into small pieces. Add salt to water.

Boil potatoes until tender. Drain, saving about ½ cup of the water with the potatoes.

Mash, add cinnamon, coconut oil and nutmeg. Mix well.

>>

Steamed Sweet Potato

INGREDIENTS

Sweet potato washed and cut into 2 inch pieces, with skin on.

DIRECTIONS

Add water to a deep pot 1/2 full. Bring water to boil on medium heat. Place the steamer on top of boiling water. Add potato to steamer. Cover and steam until tender. Enjoy!

Baked Spicy Potato

INGREDIENTS

8 medium potatoes washed
in skin
2 tablespoons olive oil
¼ teaspoon allspice powder
Black pepper to taste
Salt to taste
¼ teaspoon fennel seeds
¼ teaspoon caraway seeds
Pinch cumin

DIRECTIONS

Cut potatoes into quarters. Boil for 5 minutes. Drain and pat dry. Place all ingredients in a bowl with a lid. Shake well to coat potatoes with seasonings.

Bake in the oven at 350 degrees until tender.

>>

Smashed Potatoes

INGREDIENTS

Irish potato, washed with skin
Sweet potato, washed with skin
Carrots, washed with skin
5 fresh mint leaves minced finely
Coconut oil
Black pepper
Salt to taste

DIRECTIONS

Boil the roots together until soft and mushy, adding salt to taste. Drain, saving a bit of the water to soften up the smashed roots if it's too dry.

Smash everything together in a bowl. Mix in coconut oil. Top with mint leaves and black pepper.

Steamed Ripe Plantains or Sweet Potatoes

INGREDIENTS

Ripe plantain cut in 2 inch
thick slices, with skin
Sweet potatoes washed and
cubed

DIRECTIONS

Fill the pot with water and bring to a
boil. Place roots in a steamer and place
over boiling water. Cover and steam
until tender.

Remove the skin of the plantain.

Serve with salad, meats, veggie stew or
eat by themselves

>>>

Fingerling Potatoes

INGREDIENTS

Peeled fingerling potatoes
Swanson vegetable broth
3 strips of vegan bacon
Sliced red onion
Green thyme
Salt

DIRECTIONS

Boil potatoes in vegetable broth until
tender. Fry bacon until golden brown. Add
sliced red onion and fry until it softens.

Mix in a lot of green thyme. Add a dash of
salt (already salty from bacon). Add
potatoes with remaining vegetable broth.

Stir and simmer entire contents for 10
minutes. Top with fresh parsley.

RICES & QUINOA

Vegetable White Rice

This is a healthier version of white rice.

INGREDIENTS

2 cups white rice washed until water is clear, remove debris
1 small tomato cut small
1 tablespoon fresh rosemary leaves
1 stalk celery cut tiny
2 tablespoons butter
¼ teaspoon allspice
1 whole red chile pepper
4 whole cloves
2 cups water
¼ small onion chopped
1 fresh garlic clove minced
Salt to taste
Pinch black pepper

DIRECTIONS

Bring water to boil. Add all ingredients except red pepper. Stir well.

Bring to a boil. Lower heat to low. Toss in red pepper. Stir.

Cover, cook until tender.

>>>

Wild Rice with Quinoa

INGREDIENTS

1 cup wild rice
1 cup multicolored quinoa
Salt to taste
1 tablespoon coconut oil or butter
Fresh thyme
3 cups water

DIRECTIONS

Wash rice and quinoa. Drain. Add water to the pot. Bring to a boil. Add thyme and salt. Stir in rice and quinoa. Stir well. Lower heat to low. Cover. Once it starts to bubble, lower heat to simmer.

Cover and cook until rice is tender.

Wild Rice and Quinoa

INGREDIENTS

2 cups wild rice
1 cup tricolor quinoa
4 cups of chickpeas water or broth
Salt to taste
2 tablespoons olive coconut or olive oil
1 slice onion minced
1 clove garlic minced
1 stalk scallion minced
Pinch of black pepper
½ teaspoon dried thyme leaves
Pinch of allspice powder

DIRECTIONS

Rinse rice and quinoa well. Drain and remove any debris.

On stove top, add chickpeas water/broth to a boil on medium heat. Add all other ingredients. Stir well with a fork. Reduce heat to low, stir occasionally.

When it starts bubbling, reduce heat to low. Cook until the water is almost dried out. Reduce heat to simmer and cook for about 45 minutes.

>>>

Quinoa & Rice

INGREDIENTS

1 cup multicolored quinoa
1 cup wild rice
1 slice onion minced small
1 clove fresh garlic minced
1/4 teaspoon fresh or dried rosemary leaves
1 whole red hot pepper (do not cut)
1 teaspoon coconut oil
3 whole cloves
3 whole pimento
Salt to taste

DIRECTIONS

Wash rice and quinoa. Drain off water. Bring 4 cups of water to boil. Add all the ingredients except the whole pepper. Stir.

Bring to a boil on medium heat. Stir. Add whole pepper. Turn down the heat to low. Cover and let cook.

Turn heat to simmer when most of the water is absorbed. Let simmer until cooked.

Vegetable Rice with Lentils

Served with Turmeric & Ginger Green Beans

INGREDIENTS

2 cups rice
½ cup dried lentils washed
½ teaspoon salt
Pinch of black pepper
1 slice onion minced
1 clove garlic minced
1 slice ripe tomato minced
5 whole pimento
5 whole cloves
1 teaspoon butter
4 cups water or just enough to
cover the rice about 2 inches
above

DIRECTIONS

Wash and drain rice 3 times.

Wash and drain lentils. Remove
debris.

Add all the above in a pot. Stir.

Bring to a boil. Reduce heat to
simmer. Cook until tender and
water is dried out.

>>>

Bulgur/Quinoa Dish

INGREDIENTS
1 cup quinoa
1 cup bulgur
Dried cranberries
Cucumber
Green scallion
Almond chips
Fresh parsley
1 small tomato
Fresh mint leaves
1 handful grapes
Chop all veggies tiny.

DIRECTIONS

Cook or soak quinoa and bulgur overnight.
Mix in the chopped veggies, almond, dried
cranberries, grapes and minced mint leaves.
Pour sauce overall.

Refrigerate leftovers.

Sauce:
¼ cup lemon juice
⅓ cup olive oil
Pinch salt

SALADS & SALAD DRESSINGS

Eating your raw vegetable salad first will help you to feel full and satisfied, hence reducing your risk of overeating. Eating a raw salad daily provides fiber which is helpful to lower cholesterol, prevent colon cancer, and prevent constipation. It helps with weight loss as it keeps you feeling full longer.

Salads and fruits are micronutrients providing the necessary minerals and vitamins needed for health and a deficiency in these can lead to life-threatening health conditions.

Let's eat for health. Eat to live! Food is Life.

Ingredients to add to salads to make them more enjoyable:

- Sweet corn
- Olives
- Dried fruits (cranberries, apricots, raisins)
- Nuts of all kinds (peanuts, almond, walnuts, pecan, cashew nuts, pistachio, mixed nuts)
- Cooked beans & peas
- Mint leaves
- Seeds (whole flax, chia hemp seeds)
- Pumpkin seeds
- Fresh Fruits (avocado, grapes, apple, pineapple, berries, apples, citrus, berries, pineapple, mangoes. Whatever fruit is in season may be added to your salad for a delightful flavor)
- Quinoa
- Rice (wild rice, black rice, red rice)
- Farro
- Barley
- Roasted veggies (mushrooms, peppers, sweet potato, squashes, carrots, beets, garlic)
- Roasted, baked, or raw grated sweet potato
- Raw onions
- Raw garlic

- Raw grated carrots or beets
- Lemon or Lime juice
- Raw apple cider vinegar with the mother

Be creative with your salad so that you'll enjoy them and incorporate them in your daily diet. Skip the croutons.

Store bought salad dressings usually have unhealthy additives such as sugar that aren't good for us. Make your own salad dressings.

>>

Salad Dressing

INGREDIENTS

⅓ cup olive oil
¼ cup apple cider vinegar
2 teaspoons Dijon mustard
2 teaspoons honey
Pinch Cayenne pepper powder
1 clove fresh garlic
2 slices red onion
Pinch dried basil

DIRECTIONS

Blend all ingredients together.

May store in the refrigerator for one week.

Simple Salad Dressing

Blend everything together.

INGREDIENTS

1 small red onion
2 tablespoons Dijon mustard
2 cloves fresh garlic clove
Pinch of freshly ground black Pinch
of pepper
Pinch salt

⅓ cup Extra virgin olive oil
¼ cup raw apple cider vinegar
with the mother
1 tablespoon raw organic
unfiltered honey

>>>

Marva's Favorite Salad Dressing

INGREDIENTS

⅓ cup olive oil
¼ cup cider vinegar
2 teaspoons Dijon mustard
2 teaspoons honey
½ teaspoon salt
½ teaspoon black pepper

DIRECTIONS

Blend all ingredients
together.

May store in the
refrigerator for one week.

Marva's Homemade Salad Dressing

INGREDIENTS

Mason jar
Raw apple cider vinegar with the mother
Whole uncut cayenne or scotch bonnet peppers
Whole pimentos
Dried thyme
Fennel seeds
Ginger root
Whole uncut garlic cloves
Whole black pepper grains

DIRECTIONS

Pour everything into a mason jar. Seal. Let sit for a couple days. Drizzle on your salad as needed.

Make enough to last for a couple of weeks. No need to refrigerate.

>>>

Zucchini Salad

INGREDIENTS

Raw zucchini
Bok choy chopped tiny
Grapes
Walnuts
Raw onion minced
Black beans
Grated ginger root

DIRECTIONS

Peel and cut zucchini in small pieces

Mix all ingredients together.

Drizzle with 1 tbsp apple cider vinegar.

Creative Raw Salad One

INGREDIENTS

Italian parsley chopped
Grated raw Purple Cabbage
Raw onion sliced or minced
Chia seeds
Nuts of choice

DIRECTIONS

Mix everything together.

Drizzle with apple cider vinegar with the mother

>>

Creative Raw Salad Two

Very low calories. Tasty. Inexpensive. Keeps you feeling full.

INGREDIENTS

Parsley chopped
Bok choy cut tiny
1 Slice raw onion minced
Tomato cut tiny
Walnuts
Leaf of life leaves cut tiny (optional)
Mint of your choice minced
Callaloo/spinach leaves cut tiny

DIRECTIONS

Mix everything.

Drizzle with a little olive oil and lime/lemon juice/raw apple cider vinegar with the mother.

>>

Creative Raw Salad Three

INGREDIENTS

Italian parsley
Bok choy
Minced raw onion
Raw apple cider vinegar

DIRECTIONS

Mix everything together.

Serve with sweet potato or steamed ripe plantain.

Creative Raw Salad Four

INGREDIENTS

2 kale leaves washed and chopped
small
1/2 celery stalk washed and cut
tiny
2 Bok choy leaves washed and
chopped small
2 slices red onion minced
1 handful blueberries
1 handful dried cranberry
2 tablespoons raw apple cider
vinegar with the mother
2 tablespoons pecan oil
Optional: 2 tablespoons young
grape leaves

DIRECTIONS

Mix everything together.

Serve with baked
redskin potatoes or
steamed redskin
potatoes.

>>>

Creative Raw Salad Five

Mix everything together.

INGREDIENTS

Bok choy washed and cut tiny
Kale washed and cut tiny
2 slices raw onion minced
Handful walnuts

1 stalk scallion minced
1 stalk celery washed and cut tiny
1/8 cup grated purple cabbage
Apple cider vinegar + olive oil or
pecan oil

Quick & Easy Raw Salad

Mix everything together.

INGREDIENTS

Cucumber peeled and cut small
Bok choy washed and cut small
2 slices onion minced finely
Grated ginger root

Walnuts
Chia seeds
Lime, Lemon or
Tangerine Juice

>>

Italian Parsley Salad

INGREDIENTS

Italian parsley washed
and chopped
Raw onion minced
Raw garlic minced
Coarsely grated carrots
Walnuts
Pineapple slices

DIRECTIONS

Place parsley in a bowl. Top with grated carrots. Sprinkle minced onion and minced garlic.

Top with walnuts. Garnish with pineapple slices.

>>

Tomato & Avocado Salad

Mix everything.

INGREDIENTS

Tomatoes
Salt & pepper
Minced or slivered garlic
Avocados

Slice red onion paper thin
Balsamic vinegar/apple cider
vinegar (a tablespoon each)
½ lime juiced

Spicy Eggplant Salad

INGREDIENTS

1 eggplant washed and cut thin
1 cucumber washed, peeled
and cut small
1 small onion chopped
6 cloves fresh garlic
2 medium ripe tomato chopped
Pinch caraway seeds
Pinch fennel seeds
 2 tablespoons Jamaican spicy
curry
 1/4 teaspoon Spicy Jamaican
jerk sauce
¼ cup olive oil
4 tablespoons hot water

DIRECTIONS

Heat oil on medium. Add whole garlic and chopped onion. Fry on low heat until golden color.

Add all other ingredients. Cover and cook until tender (about 10 minutes). Stir occasionally.

Serve with steamed sweet plantain.

>>

Broccoli Salad

Mix everything together.

INGREDIENTS

Broccoli florets chopped tiny
1 tablespoon raw apple cider
vinegar with the mother
1 clove fresh garlic minced

1 slice raw onion minced finely
1 handful nuts of your choice.
½ handful dried cranberries

Spring Salad

Mix everything together. Serve with wild rice cooked with quinoa.

INGREDIENTS

1 Hass avocado cut small
2 kale leaves chopped small
2 celery stalks washed and cut small
2 slices ripe tomato cut small
2 tablespoons wild 3 leaves
Clover (optional)
1 tablespoon raw apple cider vinegar with the mother

2 tablespoons pecan oil
2 slices red onion minced
Handful walnuts
2 tablespoons dried unsweetened cranberries

>>>

Sweet Kale Salad

Mix everything together.

INGREDIENTS

Kale cut small
Broccoli florets cut small
Grated carrot
Minced raw onion
Hass avocado spooned
Grated purple cabbage
4 fresh mint leaves finely minced

4 fresh sweet basil leaves minced
Walnuts
2 tbsp raw apple cider vinegar with the mother
2 tablespoons olive, avocado or pecan oil
Handful cooked sweet corn

Avocado and Cabbage Salad

Mix everything together. Serve with baked potato, rice, or sweet potatoes.

INGREDIENTS

Shredded cabbage
1 ripe, spooned Hass avocado
1 stalk scallion minced

1 stalk celery minced
1 tbsp grated carrot
1 tbsp apple cider vinegar

>>>

Avocado & Cucumber Salad

Mix everything together. Serve with baked potato or baked sweet potato.

INGREDIENTS

Kale chopped tiny
Grated purple cabbage
Raw onion minced
Hass avocado spooned fresh
mint leaves finely minced

Apple cider vinegar
Peeled cucumber chopped
1/2 lemon

>>>>>>>>>>>>>>>>>>>>>>>>>>>>>>>>>>>>>>>

Cabbage and Lentil Salad

Mix everything together. Drizzle with a bit of apple cider vinegar, olive or pecan oil.

INGREDIENTS

2 cups cooked and drained
lentils
Grated Purple Cabbage
Pumpkin Seeds unsalted
Chia Seeds

1 stalk scallion washed and cut small
1 slice raw onion minced

Salad as a Meal

Mix everything together. Serve with black eyed peas dish and baked potato.

INGREDIENTS

2 large kale leaves washed and cut tiny
2 slices raw onion minced
¼ cup purple cabbage grated
1 ripe Hass avocado cut into cubes
6 fresh mint leaves finely minced
A few fresh moringa leaves (optional)

4 fresh grape leaves finely minced (optional)
1 tablespoon grated beetroot bulb
2 tablespoons olive oil
2 tablespoons apple cider vinegar
2 tablespoons dried unsweetened cranberries

>>

Kale & Beetroot Bush Salad

Mix everything together in a bowl. Scrape corn off the cob. Discard cob.

INGREDIENTS

Fresh kale without spine washed and chopped tiny
1 slice raw red onion minced
1 freshly cooked corn on the cob. Beetroot bush washed and chopped finely
½ freshly squeezed lemon juice
1 handful dried cranberry
1 handful walnuts

Cauliflower Salad

Mix everything together.

INGREDIENTS

Grated raw cauliflower
1 Hass avocado spooned
2 slices raw red onion
minced
1 small yellow squash
washed and grated in skin
1 small, grated carrot

1 tbsp apple cider vinegar
1 tsp olive oil
¼ cup cooked kidney beans
drained
shredded or grated raw cabbage

>>

Fresh Raw Vegetable Salad

INGREDIENTS

Fresh parsley washed
Broccoli florets washed
Tomato
1 slice onion finely minced
1 clove fresh garlic finely
minced
1 ripe Hass avocado
1 stalk celery
1/2 cucumber
Handful of unsalted
peanuts

DIRECTIONS

Cut all the vegetables into small
pieces. Place in a bowl. Drizzle with
raw organic apple cider vinegar. Top
with nuts.

May add cooked quinoa, wild rice,
brown rice. May add fruits like
chopped apples, pineapple May add
nuts, beans, peas. These will add
flavor to your salad and make it
more filling.

Collards and Beet Salad

Delicious, healthy, quick and easy.

INGREDIENTS

Collard greens chopped
finely
1 carrot
½ beetroot
1 small tomato
A few raisins

DIRECTIONS

Grate carrot and beetroot.
Mince tomato and add a few
raisins. Add collards. Mix well.

>>>

Salad with Fresh Mint Leaves

Mix everything together. OPTIONAL: You may add your favorite nuts, beans or peas like chickpeas or lentils. May add minced or grated ginger root which helps with any bloating or gas related to eating raw vegetables. Ginger also adds a nice zest to any meal, whether cooked or raw dishes.

INGREDIENTS

Raw kale chopped tiny
1 stalk Bok choy chopped tiny
1 ripe Hass avocado cut small
4 fresh mint leaves minced
Handful of fresh beetroot
leaves and stems washed and
cut up tiny
1 stalk scallion minced

1 clove fresh garlic minced
1 stalk celery cut tiny
4 tablespoon raw apple cider
vinegar
4 tablespoons pecan or olive
oil
1 handful dried unsweetened
cranberries

Tomato & Avocado Salad

Mix and serve.

INGREDIENTS

Tomatoes cut tiny
Pinch of black pepper
Balsamic vinegar/apple cider
vinegar (a tablespoon each)

Mince garlic or slice them in
slivers
Sliced red onion paper thin
½ lime juiced
Avocado cut tiny

>>

Watermelon Salad

Mix together and sprinkle a pinch of cayenne pepper powder. Cayenne adds a nice zing to any food. Its anti-inflammatory properties are well documented.

INGREDIENTS

Watermelon
Blackberries
Spinach

Grapes
Almonds

>>

Fruit & Veggie Salad

No dressing needed. Mint is a wonderful addition to any food for a delicious unique flavor. Mints have a calming effect on our bodies.

INGREDIENTS

Watermelon
Avocado
Grapes
Raspberry

Blueberries
Fresh Mint
Almonds

Broccoli & Blueberry Salad

Here you'll get a healthy meal with vegetables, fruits, nuts and grain all in one. Easy, Nutritious and delicious. Add everything together, mix well.

INGREDIENTS

Broccoli florets
Blueberries
1 slice raw minced onion
¼ fresh garlic clove minced finely
2 tablespoon raw apple cider vinegar with the mother

1 small, grated carrot
1 cup cooked lentils
1 handful walnuts
1 tbsp olive oil
1 cup quinoa or wild rice

>>>

Chickpeas & Grated Beetroot Salad

You can add any grain like quinoa to this. The beetroots give a sweet taste.

INGREDIENTS

Broccoli florets
1 beetroot bulb washed & grated

2 cups cooked chickpeas
1 Hass avocado cut into small cubes

>>

Fruit & Veggie Salad

Avocados can be a bit difficult to digest. Peppermint is a great remedy for that. Chop up and mix everything. Top with minced peppermint leaves.

INGREDIENTS

Watermelon
Grapes
Avocado
Peppermint
Peppers

Cauliflower grated
(cauliflower rice)
Blueberries
Pineapple

Chayote Squash Salad

Wash and grate squash. Squeeze lemon juice over it. Sprinkle it with a bit of chia seeds.

INGREDIENTS

½ chayote squash (grated)

1 grated yellow squash

Raw red onion (minced or sliced)

Hass avocado (spooned)

Broccoli florets

Moringa leaves (optional)

2 stalks celery cut finely

1 clove garlic clove minced finely

¼ grated carrot

1 lemon (juiced)

Chia seeds

>>>

Mushroom with Apple & Walnuts

INGREDIENTS

Mushrooms cut into halves

2 tomatoes chopped

1 onion chopped

5 whole garlic cloves

Coconut or olive oil

Pinch of salt to taste

½ red apple cubed

6 red grapes halved

¼ cup walnuts

1 cup cooked and drained

Beans of choice

½ lemon juiced

DIRECTIONS

Sauté onion, garlic, tomato. Lower heat to medium. Add mushrooms, stir. Add beans, stir. Add fruits and walnuts. Stir. Lower heat to low.

Cook until mushrooms are tender. Remove from heat.

Drizzle with lemon juice. Serve with rice, grains, or salad.

SOUPS & STEWS

Chickpeas Stew served with Wild Rice

INGREDIENTS

1 pound dried chickpeas
1 slice ginger root grated, mashed or chopped
6 ground whole allspice
6 ground whole cloves
Salt to taste
Pinch crushed red pepper
Fresh rosemary
¼ teaspoon fennel seeds
¼ teaspoon caraway seeds
Broccoli stems chopped
Fresh mint
Rosemary leaves
1 tomato chopped
1 onion chopped
4 cloves fresh garlic chopped
4 tablespoons coconut or olive oil

DIRECTIONS

Wash and drain dried chickpeas. In a large pot or pressure cooker, add chickpeas, water, allspice, cloves and salt to taste. Pressure cook until tender. Drain water. Save ¼ cup of the water/juice.

In a large pot, add oil and heat. Stir in ginger, crushed red pepper, rosemary leaves, fennel and caraway seeds, fresh mint, tomato, broccoli, garlic and onion. Lower heat to medium.

Add chickpeas and juice. Mix and simmer for about 20 minutes. Serve with wild rice and quinoa.

Pumpkin Soup

Add to a pot of water. Cook until tender and mushy. Stir often. Freeze left over.

INGREDIENTS

Lots of pumpkin squash

Carrots

Celery

Chayote squash

Onion

Garlic

Pinch salt to taste

Fresh thyme

Fresh scallion

Scotch bonnet pepper

Pumpkin flavor cock soup

Redskin potato

Sweet potatoes (optional)

Mushrooms

>>

Peanut Porridge

INGREDIENTS

Raw peanuts

Flour or oats

Coconut milk

Cinnamon

Nutmeg

Vanilla

DIRECTIONS

Blend raw peanut, flour or oats, and coconut milk until smooth. Pour this in boiling water to cook while stirring. Lower heat to simmer. When this is done, add spices like cinnamon, nutmeg, vanilla and sweeten to taste.

Eggplant Stew

Serve with your favorite starch and or salad. May add cooked lentils or cooked chickpeas to this stew.

INGREDIENTS

2 eggplants sliced diagonally then cut into squares
1 large ripe tomato
1 medium onion cut into small pieces
2 cloves fresh garlic minced
1 large carrot cut into long strips
¼ teaspoon ground pimento/allspice
¼ teaspoon crushed red pepper
½ teaspoon sea salt or seasoned salt

DIRECTIONS

Bring water to boil in a pot. Add eggplant and carrots. Cook for about 5 minutes until tender. Drain excess water. Add 1 tablespoon coconut or olive oil to the saucepan and heat on medium.

Stir in onion, garlic and tomato. Add red pepper, salt/seasoned salt, and pimento. Stir well. Add eggplant and carrots. Stir well. Turn heat to low and let simmer for about 15 minutes.

Creamy Garlic & Onion Soup

I love the flavor of this soup. Garlic and onion have natural antibiotics, so this is a great soup to consume during flu or cold seasons. It's a wonderful pick-me-upper. Flavorful, easy, cheap, and healthy.

INGREDIENTS

I head of garlic peeled and minced (about 10 cloves)
1 medium onion peeled and chopped
4 stalks scallion minced, (set aside)
1 handful Italian parsley chopped (set aside with scallion)
6 whole pimentos
4 Irish potatoes cut small, with skin on
2 cups organic vegetable stock
1 turnip bulb washed and cut small with skin on
3 tablespoons olive oil
½ teaspoon black pepper
¼ cup unsweetened coconut milk
1 carrot cut small

DIRECTIONS

In a deep pot, heat oil on low. Add onion and stir well for 1 minute. Add garlic. Stir well for 1 minute. Add potatoes, pimentos, turnips, and carrots.

Fill the pot halfway with water. Add stock. Bring to a boil. Cook for about 30 minutes. Turn off the stove and let cool.

Once cool. Pour into the blender. Add scallion and parsley. Blend until creamy. Pour back into the pot. Turn heat to low.

Stir in coconut milk and black pepper. Simmer for 5 minutes. Top with shredded Italian parsley and minced scallion.

It's Soup Day

Add all ingredients to the chickpeas water. Stir. Cook on low until veggies are tender.

INGREDIENTS

1 pack of chickpeas washed and cooked until tender. Save the chickpeas water. Do not discard.
2 stalks celery chopped
1 small onion chopped
4 cloves fresh garlic chopped
fresh thyme
2 stalks scallion chopped
2 cups cabbage chopped

1 pint mushrooms washed and chopped
6 whole pimento grains
2 slices ginger root minced
1 carrot sliced lengthwise
¼ tsp crushed red pepper
Salt to taste
pinch of black pepper

>>

Vegetable Soup

Chop all the vegetables. Cook everything together for about 1 hour. Top with fennel seeds and sliced avocado. Salt to taste.

INGREDIENTS

Black eyed peas
Zucchini squash
Cucumber
Carrots
Cabbage
Bell pepper
Mushrooms

Onion chopped
Garlic chopped and whole
Celery chopped
Thyme
Whole pimento
Crushed red pepper to taste
2 slices of minced ginger root

Jamaican Spicy Jerk Veggie Stew

INGREDIENTS

1 cup chopped cabbage

1 cup chopped eggplant

1 carrot sliced lengthwise

1 medium onion chopped

6 cloves fresh garlic (do not cut)

1 ripe tomato chopped

1 cup cooked beans of choice

¼ cup coconut milk

1 cup string beans washed and cut into 1 inch strips. Remove stems.

1 tablespoon hot jerk sauce

1/4 teaspoon allspice powder

2 tablespoon coconut oil

DIRECTIONS

In a large pot, heat oil on low. Add peeled garlic. Roast until golden. Add other ingredients. Stir and mix well. Cover and cook on low until string beans are tender.

Serve with *Steamed Sweet Potato.*

>>

Broccoli, Chickpeas, Cucumber Stew

Heat oil. Add all ingredients. Stir. Simmer until cooked.

INGREDIENTS

Broccoli cut up

Carrots cut up

Cucumber cut small bits

Cooked and drained chickpeas (save ¼ cup of the juice)

1 onion chopped

5 cloves garlic chopped

Salt to taste

Crushed red pepper

Pinch of allspice

Pinch of clove powder

3 tablespoons coconut oil

1 ripe tomato chopped

Meatless Red Peas Soup Jamaican Style

INGREDIENTS

Pumpkin (calabaza squash)
1 cup of red peas
1 yellow yam
2 carrots chopped up
1 diced sweet potato (the white one)
Corn on the cob
A few dumplings
1 onion
Fresh thyme
Scallion
Garlic
Soup seasoning

DIRECTIONS

Boil the pumpkin until it breaks apart completely. In the meantime, pressure cook red peas. Add peas to the pumpkin.

Add yellow yam, chopped carrots, diced sweet potato, corn on the cob, and a few dumplings. Add salt, onion, fresh thyme, scallion, garlic and soup seasoning.

>>>

Yellow Pumpkin Stew

Add everything to a pot. Stir. Reduce heat and simmer until tender.

INGREDIENTS

Yellow pumpkin with skin on, cut into small cubes
Butternut squash with skin on, cut into small cubes
Cauliflower cut small
Broccoli cut small

1 large Onion chopped small
4 cloves fresh Garlic cut small
1 ripe Tomato chopped
Fresh or dry thyme leaves
¼ tsp salt or to taste
Olive or coconut oil
pinch black pepper

Butternut Squash & Broccoli Stew

INGREDIENTS

1 medium onion chopped
4 cloves fresh garlic minced
1 tomato chopped
Salt/seasoning salt to taste
Crushed red pepper to taste
Butternut squash washed, cut into small cubes, with skin on
Broccoli stem and florets cut into small bits
Coconut or olive oil
¼ cup water

DIRECTIONS

Heat oil. Add onion, garlic, and tomato stir. Add salt and pepper. Stir. Reduce heat to low.

Add butternut squash. Stir. Add water. Cover and simmer until squash is halfway cooked. Stir in broccoli.

Cook on low heat until squash is tender. Serve with rice, quinoa, or baked potatoes.

>>

Veggie Stew

INGREDIENTS

String beans
Onion
Garlic
Tomato
¼ teaspoon jerk sauce
¼ cup water
Mushrooms
2 tablespoon coconut oil
Carrots
Zucchini

DIRECTIONS

Cut all veggies into small pieces. Heat oil. Add all the ingredients. Stir.

Add water. Stir. Simmer until tender. Salt to taste

Serve with fried sweet plantain.

Meatless Chili

INGREDIENTS

1 ½ pounds of cooked lentils
1 pack of chili seasoning
Chili powder
3 8oz cans of tomato sauce (1
of each flavor)
2 small cans of flavored
tomato paste
1 can of diced tomatoes (do
not drain)
2 cans of red kidney beans
Diced green peppers
1 small, diced onion
2 cloves diced garlic
Cayenne pepper
Optional toppings: shredded
vegan cheese
Sour cream
1 diced jalapeno

DIRECTIONS

Season lentils with black pepper,
seasoning salt and powdered garlic.
Cook for 10-15 minutes until brown
(use spatula to stir lentil so it doesn't
get lumpy). Drain excess water.

Combine lentils with all of the above.
Bring to a boil, then simmer on low
heat for 20 minutes (stir periodically
to prevent sticking to the pot).

Great with saltines, or plain white
rice.

Meatless Jamaican Stew Peas

This can be an occasional treat dish; hence you can use canned beans for convenience.

INGREDIENTS

Salt fish/Salted codfish
4 Large cans red beans
1/2 red bell pepper
½ yellow bell pepper
1 medium onion
3 fresh garlic cloves
1 red scotch bonnet pepper
1 whole red scotch bonnet pepper
1 whole green scotch bonnet pepper
8 ounces coconut milk
1 stick margarine or butter
Scallion
Thyme
Black pepper to taste
10 whole Uncrushed pimentos/allspice
White flour for spinners dumplings

DIRECTIONS

Spinners recipe below.

Chop peppers, onion, and scallion.

Boil Saltfish until tender. Pour off the water. Taste the inner part of the salt fish to make sure that all the salt is not removed. It needs to be a bit salty to taste. Remove bones if this is salt fish with bones or if you prefer, you may leave the bones. Break up saltfish into small pieces.

In a large pot sauté butter, onion, garlic, scallion. Save the whole peppers. Stir in saltfish.

Add coconut milk and stir. Add red beans. Stir. Add thyme and black pepper. Cover. Reduce heat to simmer.

Pour white flour into a bowl. Add cold water to flour and knead into a dough. Pinch off small pieces of flour dough and roll between your palms to make elongated dumplings called spinners or rolli polli dumplings. Add the dumplings and gently stir.

Toss in whole scotch bonnet peppers. Toss in whole pimentos. Gently stir. Cover and let simmer until dumplings are cooked and stew has thickened.

If the juice is not thick enough, make a paste with cold water and flour, add to stew and stir, let cook for a few minutes. Enjoy over white rice.

Obe Stew (Nigerian dish)

This stew is typically made with a combo of 3 meats: oxtail, turkey, goat, beef tripe, stock fish etc.

If making with stock fish, boil the fish separately for 1-1.5 hours. Otherwise, boil all meat together with ½ - 1 bouillon cube, iodine salt, ½ an onion for about 1 - 1 ½ hours until soft.

INGREDIENTS

Possible meats: oxtail, turkey, goat, beef tripe, stock fish

6 plum tomatoes
3 red peppers
4-4 ½ red scotch bonnet peppers
4-5 fresh garlic cloves
1 chopped onion

(Blend all of these together with ½ cup stock from the boiled meats and fish.)

DIRECTIONS

Wash the meat. Use ½ cup of stock from the boiled meat to blend with the vegetables.

Heat olive oil in a pot. When hot, add the blended mix, boiled meat, 1 cup of meat stock, boiled stockfish, cook together for 45 mins. Add iodized salt.

Keep watching to make sure the sauce doesn't get too thick. If getting thick, add a little water.

Chickpeas Stew

INGREDIENTS

1 pound dried chickpeas
½ pound mushrooms
2 large white potatoes
1 small sweet potato
1 medium onion
2 cloves fresh garlic
1 medium ripe tomato
½ teaspoon allspice powder
½ teaspoon fresh ground red pepper
A pinch of ground cloves
1 teaspoon dried or fresh rosemary leaves
½ teaspoon dried or fresh mint leaves
2 slices fresh ginger root cut into tiny bits
1 tablespoon butter
Salt or seasoning salt to taste
A pinch of black pepper

DIRECTIONS

Wash chickpeas and pressure or slow cook until tender. Save the juice/water. Cut up all vegetables. Set aside. Wash potatoes. Leave skin on. Cut into cubes. Wash and cut mushrooms into quarters.

In a large pot, add cooked chickpeas in its water. Place on medium heat. Stir in potatoes. Bring to a boil. Add all the vegetables, spices, seasonings, and butter. Stir well.

Cook on low heat until potatoes are halfway cooked. Stir in mushrooms. Cook on low heat until potatoes are tender. This is a one pot meal but can be served with anything.

VEGETABLES

And God said, "Behold, I have given you every plant yielding seed that is on the face of all the earth, and every tree with seed in its fruit. You shall have them for food. Genesis 1:29 ESV

If weight loss is your goal, include lots of vegetables in your diet and minimize the heavy carbs like potato, pasta and processed foods.

A great kitchen investment is an aluminum steamer that can be placed over a pot of boiling water to steam vegetables and roots.

By cooking potatoes, roots, and yams in water, we lose some of its nutritional value. Try steaming them instead.

>>>

Steamed not Fried Sweet Ripe Plantains

You may eat the cooked plantain with or without the skin. Serve with any of the sautéed vegetable or bean dishes recipes in this book. If you're a meat eater, this is a nice healthy compliment to any meat dish.

INGREDIENTS

Ripe plantain washed

DIRECTIONS

Leaving skin on, cut diagonally to your choice of size. Place water in a pot, bring to boil. Place the steamer on top of the boiling water. Cover and steam until tender.

Beetroot

Beetroots are rich in iron, vitamin C and folate.

Sautéed Beetroot Bush

INGREDIENTS

1 to 2 bunches of beetroot bush including stems.
1 large onion chopped
1 large tomato chopped
4 cloves garlic bulbs cut small
Pinch of salt to taste
4 tbsp olive oil
1 red pepper chopped

DIRECTIONS

Cut beetroots into 1 inch strips. Heat olive oil in a pot. Add all vegetables except beetroot. Sauté. Stir in beetroot bush. Stir. Cover and simmer for about 10 minutes. Serve over rice, quinoa, or any grain.

>>

Sautéed Beetroots

INGREDIENTS

1 medium beetroot bulb washed
1 small onion chopped small
4 cloves fresh garlic minced
1 cup steamed, drained and chopped cauliflower
1 cup cooked and drained lentils
Salt to taste
1/2 teaspoon spicy Jamaican jerk sauce
1 pinch allspice powder
4 tablespoons olive oil

DIRECTIONS

Cut beetroots into 1 inch strips. Leave skin on. Heat oil on medium low. Add garlic and fry until golden brown. Mix in onion. Cook until tender. Mix in all other ingredients.

Cabbage

INGREDIENTS

½ small red cabbage chopped
small
2 cups cooked string beans cut into
½ inch strips. Drain off water, save
1 cup full of the water
2 stalks celery cut into small pieces
1 large carrot cut lengthwise into
small strips
1 large onion chopped
3 cloves fresh garlic cloves
chopped
1 large tomato chopped
½ red, green or yellow sweet
pepper chopped
Salt or seasoning salt to taste
Crushed red pepper to taste
Your favorite cooking oil

DIRECTIONS

In a large skillet, heat oil. Stir in
onion, garlic, tomato, sweet
pepper, salt and pepper. Stir
well

Add all other vegetables. Stir
well. Pour the saved string
beans water, stir. Reduce heat
to low.

Simmer until vegetables are
cooked. Serve with baked
potato, rice or any healthy
grains/carbs or just by itself.

Cabbage & Mushroom Stir Fry

INGREDIENTS

1/2 small cabbage washed and
chopped small
1 packet organic whole mushrooms
washed and halved
1 small onion chopped small
8 cloves of fresh garlic, do not cut.
1 ripe tomato cut small
2 slices ginger root minced
1 pinch pimento powder
¼ teaspoon salt/seasoning salt
1 pinch black pepper
1 pinch crushed red pepper
⅛ cup olive oil

DIRECTIONS

Heat oil on medium. Add ginger
and whole garlic. Fry gently
until brownish.

Stir in onion, tomato, pimento
powder, salt, and peppers. Stir
in cabbage. Reduce heat to low.

Stir in mushrooms. Cover and
let simmer for about 10
minutes.

Serve with roasted or baked
sweet potato or wild rice.

>>>

Cabbage & Mushrooms

INGREDIENTS

2 cups cabbage washed and
chopped
1 cup mushrooms halved
1 small onion chopped
4 whole cloves fresh garlic
1 slice ginger root minced
1 small ripe tomato chopped
¼ bell pepper chopped
2 tablespoon olive oil
Pinch salt to taste
¼ teaspoon crushed red pepper

DIRECTIONS

Heat oil on medium. Stir in all
ingredients. Reduce heat to
low. Simmer until cabbage
tender.

This is a low calorie, healthy
dish that will help you with
your weight loss goals. Serve
with baked potato and a raw
green salad.

Jerk Any Veggies Kinda Dinner

INGREDIENTS

Green or purple cabbage cut up
small
Eggplant washed, cut up small
1 small onion chopped
2 fresh garlic cloves minced
¼ bell pepper chopped
1 slice ginger root minced
1 medium ripe tomato chopped
2 tablespoons coconut oil
2 tablespoons olive oil
1 teaspoon spicy Jamaican jerk
sauce

DIRECTIONS

Heat oils on medium heat.
Add garlic and fry until
golden.

Add jerk sauce. Stir. Add
everything else. Lower heat
to low. Stir well.

Cover and let simmer until
cooked. Stir occasionally.

>>

Sautéed Cabbages & Mixed Veggies

INGREDIENTS

Chopped purple cabbage
Chopped green cabbage
½ onion chopped
6 whole garlic peeled
1 medium ripe tomato chopped
Leftover kale spine cut small
2 tablespoons olive oil
Pinch of salt to taste
Pinch crushed red pepper to taste
¼ teaspoon fennel seeds
4 tablespoons water

DIRECTIONS

Heat oil on medium. Fry whole
garlic until golden brown. Add
all ingredients. Stir well.

Reduce heat to low. Simmer
until tender (about 10
minutes).

Cauliflower

Easy Cauliflower Recipe

INGREDIENTS

Cauliflower
Parsley
Thyme
Green onion
Paprika
Pinch salt and pepper

DIRECTIONS

Cauliflower cooked and drained. Add fresh parsley, thyme and green onion for taste. Add paprika and a pinch salt and pepper.

Roast in the oven.

>>

Sautéed cauliflower

INGREDIENTS

½ cut and steamed cauliflower, chopped small
1 teaspoon fennel seeds
¼ cup olive oil
Pinch allspice powder
1 slice ginger root minced
4 cloves fresh garlic chopped
½ onion chopped
1 large ripe tomato chopped
Salt to taste
Pinch black pepper

DIRECTIONS

Heat oil on medium heat. Add garlic and fry until golden brown. Add fennel seeds, onion, salt, pepper, tomato, ginger root, allspice. Stir.

Add cauliflower. Reduce heat to low. Simmer for about 15 minutes.

Cauliflower Sautéed in Olive Oil

INGREDIENTS

Chopped fresh garlic cloves
Onion
Tomato
Crushed red pepper
Salt to taste

DIRECTIONS

Sauté. Top with slices of steamed butternut squash and several pieces of steamed carrot.

>>>

Cauliflower Rice

INGREDIENTS

1 head cauliflower washed, dried, grated
1 small onion minced
2 cloves fresh garlic minced
¼ red bell pepper chopped small
¼ cup corn
¼ cup peas
2 stalks scallion cut small
¼ teaspoon fennel seeds
¼ teaspoon grated ginger root
1 cup broccoli florets
1 large onion coarsely grated
4 tablespoons olive oil

DIRECTIONS

Heat oil on medium in a large skillet. Add onion and garlic, fry until golden brown.

Stir in all other ingredients. Reduce heat to low. Cover and cook for about 10 minutes. Stir occasionally.

INGREDIENTS

1 head cauliflower
1 teaspoon Jamaican jerk sauce
3 teaspoons Jamaican curry powder
Pinch black pepper
¼ cup curry paste
½ teaspoon grated ginger root
¼ teaspoon crushed red pepper
¼ teaspoon caraway seeds
¼ teaspoon cumin powder
4 tablespoons olive oil

DIRECTIONS

Combine all the ingredients in a bowl and mix to a paste. Cut cauliflower in small pieces. Remove leaves. Rub paste all over cauliflower.

Heat oven to 350 degrees. Line the baking tin with foil paper. Baste foil paper with olive oil.

Place cauliflower on the baking tin. Drizzle olive oil over cauliflower.

Bake until tender, about 45 minutes to 1 hour

Eggplant

Eggplant Dish

INGREDIENTS

1 large eggplant
1 medium onion chopped small
1 carrot into lengthwise into small strips
3 cloves fresh garlic cut small
1 medium ripe tomato cut small
½ sweet pepper cut small
1 slice fresh ginger cut into small bits
Salt/seasoning salt to taste
Crushed red peppers to taste
Allspice to taste
Oil of choice

DIRECTIONS

Wash and cut eggplant into small size cubes. Heat oil. Add onion, garlic, tomato, sweet pepper, ginger, salt, allspice, crushed red pepper. Stir and sauté on medium heat for 3 minutes. Add carrots and eggplant. Stir well. Cover.

Reduce heat to low and let cook until eggplant and carrots are tender. Cooks in about 10 minutes. Serve over rice or any other grains or roots.

>>

Easy Eggplant Stew

INGREDIENTS

Chickpeas cooked
Onion
Garlic
Tomato
Crushed red pepper
Salt to taste
Mushrooms

DIRECTIONS

Mix everything, cook until eggplant is tender (tastes like meat).

INGREDIENTS

1 small cucumber cut into cubes
1 large tomato cut small pieces
1 large onion chopped
4 cloves fresh garlic minced

½ eggplant cut into small cubes
1 slice ginger minced
4 tablespoons olive oil
¼ teaspoon seasoning salt
Pinch crushed red pepper
1 cup yellow squash cubed

DIRECTIONS

In a large pot, heat olive oil. Add onion, garlic, tomato, salt, pepper. Stir and sauté. Add all other vegetables. Stir well. Cover and simmer until tender. Serve with Vegetable Rice (recipe included in this book).

>>

Sautéed Eggplant and Greens

INGREDIENTS

Cooked frozen green beans
Mustard greens washed and chopped
Eggplant washed and cut small
1 small onion chopped
3 cloves fresh garlic minced
1 medium ripe tomato chopped
¼ teaspoon allspice powder
¼ teaspoon spicy Jamaican jerk sauce
Pinch salt to taste
4 tablespoons coconut oil
2 tablespoons olive oil

DIRECTIONS

Sauté everything on low heat until tender.

Serve with quinoa wild rice, roasted sweet potato or your favorite starch in small portions.

Note that you can be quite creative with your vegetables. Add any of your favorite seasoning and spices to give it a nice kick.

Squash

Finger Lickin Good!

INGREDIENTS

Spaghetti squash washed
and halved
1 onion finely chopped
4 cloves fresh garlic minced
2 large ripe tomato cut
small
1 small carrot cut into tiny,
long strips
1 teaspoon thyme leaves
Pinch cumin
Pinch coriander
1 slice ginger root cut tiny
bits
1 teaspoon
allspice/pimento powder
Pinch powdered clove
1 teaspoon seasoning salt
¼ teaspoon crushed red
pepper

DIRECTIONS

Cook spaghetti squash in a conventional oven for about 30 minutes at 400 degrees. Or boil in a pot full of water for 30 minutes or microwave until tender.

Scoop the seeds out and save to snack on (healthy). Scoop the inside of the squash and set aside. Save that shell/skin intact to be used as your bowl.

In a large pot sauté all other ingredients. Add a bit of water if needed so it doesn't dry out. Mix in squash. Simmer for 10 minutes.

Spoon this inside the shell of the spaghetti squash which serves as your bowl.

OPTIONAL: Add some steamed sweet potatoes and a handful of walnuts on top.

Spaghetti Squash Dish

INGREDIENTS

1 spaghetti squash cut in half
1 medium onion chopped
small
1 ripe tomato chopped small
4 cloves fresh garlic minced
2 tablespoons curry powder
¼ tsp jerk sauce
4 tablespoons coconut oil
2 sliced ginger root cut tiny
¼ red sweet pepper chopped
small

DIRECTIONS

Place water in a wide pot. Bring to a boil. Place squash cut side up. Steam until tender. Drain water. Scoop spaghetti out and set aside. Heat oil on medium. Stir in curry and jerk sauce. Add onion, tomato, garlic, pepper, ginger root. Reduce heat to low. Stir well. Add spaghetti squash. Stir well. Lower heat to simmer. Cook for 10 minutes. Enjoy by itself or with a salad, potato, or grains.

>>

Sautéed Butternut Squash & Broccoli

INGREDIENTS

Butternut squash thinly sliced
with skin on
Broccoli florets and stems cut in
small pieces
1 medium onion chopped
2 cloves fresh garlic chopped
1 small tomato chopped
Sea salt or seasoning salt to taste
2 tablespoons coconut oil
4 ounces water
¼ teaspoon crushed red pepper

DIRECTIONS

In a large saucepan, place coconut oil and heat on medium heat. Stir in onion, garlic, tomato, salt/seasoning salt to taste, crushed red pepper. Add sliced butternut squash. Stir. Add water. Stir. Cook until tender. Add broccoli. Stir and simmer on low heat until broccoli is slightly tender. Do not overcook broccoli. Serve over wild rice, quinoa, bulgur, spelt, barley, or farro (these are healthy grains). May also serve with cooked lentil or chickpeas.

Mushrooms

INGREDIENTS

Mushrooms
Onion chopped
Garlic minced
Tomato chopped
Red sweet pepper
Brussel sprouts halved
1 cup cooked red kidney beans
Pinch fennel seeds
Pinch of caraway seeds
Pinch salt to taste
2 slices scotch bonnet pepper
minced
Olive or coconut oil
Pinch allspice powder

DIRECTIONS

Heat oil on low. Stir in garlic, stir and cook until slightly golden brown. Add onion, tomato, and sweet pepper. Stir well. Add caraway, fennel, salt, and allspice. Stir well.

Add all other ingredients, stir well. Cover and simmer for 10 minutes.

INGREDIENTS

2 stalks fresh celery chopped, small pieces
1 pound cooked chickpeas (save the water)
1 medium onion chopped
3 cloves garlic chopped
½ red bell pepper chopped
1 tomato chopped
2 slices ginger root minced finely
8 oz organic mushrooms washed and chopped
¼ teaspoon crushed red pepper
¼ teaspoon fennel seeds
Seasoning/Sea salt to taste
Pinch of powdered allspice
Pinch of clove powder
Olive or coconut oil

DIRECTIONS

Heat oil in a large skillet. Add onion, garlic, tomato, red sweet pepper, ginger, and fennel seeds.

Stir in seasoning salt, allspice, clove, crushed red pepper. Stir in remaining ingredients. Lower heat to medium.

Add about ¼ cup of the saved chickpeas water. Stir. Reduce heat and sauté for about 10 minutes or until mushrooms are tender.

Serve with rice, quinoa, fried sweet plantains, boiled ripe plantain or any of your favorite grains, or eat just by itself.

Zucchini

Sautéed Zucchini & Peppers

Chop all veggies into small pieces. Sauté together on low until the zucchini is slightly tender.

INGREDIENTS

Coconut oil
Zucchini
Onion
Garlic
Tomato

Mushroom
Yellow bell pepper
Crushed red pepper
Salt to taste
Ginger root

>>>>>>>>>>>>>>>>>>>>>>>>>>>>>>>>>>>>>>>

Mint & Ginger Mushrooms with Zucchini

INGREDIENTS

1 packet fresh mushroom
1 large zucchini
1 large onion
2 cloves fresh garlic cloves minced
1 large tomato
Fresh ginger root minced finely or grated
Fresh or dry mint leaves of choice, cut into tiny pieces
Seasoning salt to taste
Crushed red pepper to taste
Cooking oil of choice

DIRECTIONS

Cut up all the vegetables into small bits. Separate zucchini. Sprinkle seasoning salt onto zucchini and mix well. Heat oil in a pot. Add onion, garlic, tomato, ginger, mint and stir. Turn heat to low. Add zucchini and stir. Fold in mushrooms. Sprinkle it with crushed pepper. Stir well. Turn heat to simmer and let cook until vegetables are tender. Do not overcook.

Mushrooms produce a lot of juice when cooked.

Other Vegetable Dishes

Meatless Collard Greens

INGREDIENTS

1 bag cut collards
1 large onion chopped
4 cloves freshly cut garlic
1 tomato
6 whole cloves
6 whole pimento/allspice
¼ teaspoon salt
¼ teaspoon crushed red pepper
1 packet mushrooms
1 tablespoon butter

DIRECTIONS

Wash collards and drain. Place all ingredients in a pot. Add 2 cups of water. Cook on low heat for about 2 hours until tender. Drink the liquid as a soup/broth.

>>>>>>>>>>>>>>>>>>>>>>>>>>>>>>>>>>>>>>>

Quick Sautéed Spinach

INGREDIENTS

Garlic
Red onion
Coconut oil
Baby spinach
Himalayan pink sea salt
Black pepper

DIRECTIONS

Cut up garlic and red onion, sauté together in coconut oil until the garlic gets brown and the onion softens. Add a few handfuls of baby spinach, add Himalayan pink sea salt and black pepper. Drizzle with a little more coconut oil. Mix together and sauté for another 6-7 mins on medium heat until spinach wilts down.

This dish is filled with Vitamin C, Vitamin A, and minerals including iron. Sauté everything together until tender for about 30 minutes on low heat. Serve with baked or steamed sweet potato, cooked potato, rice or corn bread.

INGREDIENTS

Mustard greens washed and chopped

Turnip greens with stems washed and chopped

2 turnip bulbs washed and cut small

1 large onion chopped

4 cloves fresh garlic chopped

½ yellow bell pepper chopped

2 ripe tomato chopped

Salt to your taste

Pinch black pepper

Pinch crushed red pepper

Pinch allspice powder

3 tablespoons coconut oil

3 tablespoons olive oil

¼ cup water

>>>

Sautéed Mixed Veggies

Sauté until tender, do not overcook.

INGREDIENTS

Mushrooms

Purple Cabbage chopped

Onion

Garlic

Tomato

Yellow sweet pepper

Caraway seeds

Salt to taste

Crushed red pepper

Sliced minced ginger

Olive or coconut oil

INGREDIENTS

10 pieces of okra
Orange or green scotch
bonnet pepper
½ bouillon cube
Fish stock (optional)
Salt to taste.

DIRECTIONS

Blend okra together with 1 orange or green scotch bonnet pepper and half bouillon cube, and fish stock. Add blended mix to a saucepan.

Add pieces of cooked fish (no bones): blue fish, crayfish, dried shrimp etc. Add salt.

Cook for 10 mins on low heat, stir often.

>>

Oven Roasted Corn on The Cob

You may add any of your favorite powdered spices including powdered onion or garlic to make your corn as delicious as ever.

INGREDIENTS

Corn on the cob, remove husk
Olive oil
Salt or seasoning salt to taste
Black pepper
Pinch cayenne pepper
Pinch paprika
Allspice powder
Pinch of Cinnamon Powder

DIRECTIONS

Coat corn well with olive oil. Place in a large rectangular baking tray. Mix all other ingredients in a bowl. Using your fingers, rub the mixed spices onto the oiled corn on the cob.

Preheat the oven to 350 degrees. Bake on the top shelf of the oven for 30 minutes. Using a long fork, turn the corn after 15 minutes.

INGREDIENTS

6 mushrooms washed & halved
6 Brussel sprouts washed and halved
1 small onion chopped
4 garlic cloves chopped
1 small ripe tomato chopped
1 cup cooked chickpeas
½ cup chickpeas water or vegetable broth
1 handful chopped cabbage
¼ cup corn
1 medium carrot cut thinly lengthwise
4 tablespoons coconut or olive oil
Pinch salt to taste
¼ tsp black pepper
¼ tsp allspice powder
Pinch caraway seeds

DIRECTIONS

On medium heat, fry garlic until golden brown. Add spices and seasonings. Stir in all the veggies. Stir well.

Add broth or chickpeas water. Mix well. Reduce heat to low. Cook until carrots are tender.

Serve with a raw veggie salad.

Note: mushroom makes any vegetable dish taste like meat and is a delightful addition to any sautéed vegetable or stewed vegetables.

INGREDIENTS

6 whole mushrooms washed
½ yellow sweet pepper chopped
4 cloves fresh garlic minced
1 small onion chopped
1 cup cooked and drained chickpeas
1 small ripe tomato chopped
½ cup chopped purple cabbage
Salt to taste
Pinch black pepper
¼ teaspoon allspice powder
4 tablespoons olive or coconut oil
1 kale leaf with stem chopped
1 tablespoon fresh thyme

DIRECTIONS

Heat oil on medium. Stir in garlic, fry until golden brown. Lower heat to low. Add onion, tomato, salt, sweet pepper, thyme, allspice, black pepper. Stir.

Add all other ingredients. Stir. Cover and simmer for about 10 minutes.

Serve with baked potato, rice, quinoa or boiled corn on the cob or your favorite healthy carb.

DINNER TODAY

Incorporating more vegetables, fruits, nuts, seeds and grains can help you to lose that excess weight and keep it off, leading to a healthier and stronger you. Eating this way can also help to prevent or reverse debilitating health conditions.

Try any of these recipes as a complete meal.

Meat alternatives

Sauté mushrooms, red kidney beans, red onion, garlic cloves, broccoli stalks, tomato, red bell peppers, pinch of salt, spicy pepper, olive oil.

One Pot Meal

Heat oil on medium. Add curry, jerk sauce, and allspice. Stir. Lower heat to low. Stir in vegetables. Cover and simmer until tender.

INGREDIENTS

Brussel sprouts washed and cut in half
Sweet plantains peeled and cut into small pieces
Beet bulbs washed and cut into small pieces
Spinach
Carrots washed and cut into thin strips
Sweet potato washed and cut into small cubes
1 whole scotch bonnet pepper
Mushroom washed and cut into halves
1 slice Ginger root minced
1 Onion chopped
Red or yellow bell peppers chopped
1 tablespoon spicy Jamaican curry powder
1 teaspoon spicy Jamaican jerk sauce
Pinch allspice powder
Coconut oil

Meatless Chili

INGREDIENTS

1 tablespoon olive oil
6 cloves garlic, minced
1 medium onion, chopped
1 medium red bell pepper,
chopped
1 scotch bonnet pepper,
chopped
1 teaspoon sea salt
¼ teaspoon black pepper
1 crushed red pepper
4 tablespoons chili powder
1 tablespoon cumin
4 tomatoes, chopped
1 can tomato paste
4 cups vegetable broth
2 cups water
1 ½ cups red quinoa
1 cup red kidney bean,
drained
1 cup pinto bean, drained
1 cup black beans, cooked
and drained
1 tablespoon freshly
squeezed lemon juice
1 teaspoon dried oregano
1 tablespoon fresh cilantro

DIRECTIONS

In a large pot, add oil, garlic, onion, pepper, scotch bonnet pepper, salt, cayenne pepper, chili powder, and cumin. Sauté everything until tender.

Add tomato paste and chopped tomato, vegetable broth, water, quinoa, kidney beans, pinto beans, and black beans. Bring to a boil. Cover and simmer for 30 minutes.

Add corn, lime juice, oregano, and cilantro, cook on low for 5 minutes.

Sautéed Lentils, Potato, Plantain, & Salad Dinner

INGREDIENTS

2 cups cooked and drained
lentils
1 small onion chopped
6 cloves fresh garlic cut small
bits
2 small ripe tomatoes
chopped
1 stalk scallion chopped
¼ cups olive oil
1 tsp fennel seeds
3 redskin potatoes washed,
leave skin on
1 very ripe plantain washed,
leave skin on
1 carrot washed, cut, leave
skin on
1 tbsp olive oil for mashed
potato

Raw Salad:

2 stalks Bok choy cut small
1 stalk scallion cut tiny
2 slices raw onion minced
1 teaspoon chia seeds
1 tsp freshly squeezed lemon
juice
1 Hass avocado cut into small
bits

DIRECTIONS

Heat oil on medium. Add garlic, fry
until golden brown. Stir in onions,
tomato, scallion, fennel seeds.
Reduce heat to low. Add lentils. Stir.
Sauté for 5 minutes, stirring
occasionally.

Boil or steam potatoes, plantain, and
carrot together. When cooked, place
in a bowl and mash together. Mix in
olive oil. If too dry, add 3 tbsp hot
water and mix.

Mix together.

Rice and Salad Dinner

Rice INGREDIENTS

1 cup white rice washed 3 times and drained
1 cup water
Thyme
1 stalk scallion
Pinch salt
1 teaspoon olive oil

Salad INGREDIENTS

Washed and grated cauliflower
1 Haas avocado spooned
2 stalks Bok choy chopped
1 stalk scallion/green onion chopped
2 slices raw onion minced
¼ lemon juiced

Rice DIRECTIONS

Mix everything. Cook on low heat until tender.

Mix salad ingredients together.

>>

Squash and Sweet Potato Dinner

INGREDIENTS

Turnip greens
Raw onion
Pumpkin seeds
Spicy curry powder
Fennel seeds
Ginger root
Steamed sweet potato

Garlic
Tomato
Turnip bulb cut small
Bell pepper
Scotch bonnet pepper
Yellow squash cubed
Chayote squash peeled & cubed

Steamed Potato and Beetroot with Kale Salad Dinner

Starch INGREDIENTS

1 Irish potato (unpeeled)
1 beetroot (unpeeled)

Salad INGREDIENTS

4 kale leaves. Remove spine and save.
Bush and leaves from 1 beetroot
2 slices red onion minced
Handful of mixed nuts
2 cups cooked and drained lentils
½ freshly juiced lime
1 tablespoon raw apple cider Vinegar with the mother

DIRECTIONS

Wash and cut Irish potatoes in small cubes. Wash and cut beetroot in cubes. Steam in a steamer.

Salad DIRECTIONS

Wash kale leaves. Chop very small.

Wash and drain beetroot leaves. Cut small.

Mix everything together.

Cauliflower/Potatoes & Mushrooms Dinner

INGREDIENTS

Cauliflower Mushrooms
Zucchini
1 tomato
1 onion
2 redskin potatoes
2 cloves fresh garlic
Salt to taste
Seasoning salt to taste
¼ teaspoon crushed red pepper
Oil of your choice

DIRECTIONS

Wash and steam cauliflower until tender. Drain. Cut into small pieces and set aside. Wash mushrooms and cut into small pieces, set aside. Wash and cut zucchini into small, thin slices. Set aside. Wash and cut potatoes into small, thin slices. Leave skin on. Set aside.

Sprinkle with seasoning salt to taste. Chop onion, garlic, tomatoes.

Heat oil in a large pot. Add potatoes and stir. Add onion, garlic and tomatoes. Stir. Add zucchini, stir. Toss in mushrooms and cauliflower. Sprinkle crushed pepper. Stir. Reduce heat to low.

Cook until potatoes are tender. If additional juice is needed to cook the potatoes, add a spoonful of the cauliflower water.

Veggie Dinner

INGREDIENTS

1 small/medium cabbage
1 small/medium onion
3-5 cloves garlic
1 whole or 2-4 Roma tomato
Ginger root
Salt
1-2 tablespoons coconut oil

SALAD INGREDIENTS

Italian parsley chopped small
4 leaves Bok choy chopped tiny
Apple cider vinegar & olive oil
for dressing
Sweet potato
Walnuts
Cinnamon powder

POTATO DIRECTIONS

Chop all veggies. Steam cabbage
with onion, garlic, tomato, sliced
ginger root minced, pinch salt, a
little coconut oil.

Salad DIRECTIONS

Drizzle with apple cider vinegar
and 1 tablespoon olive oil.

Cook sweet potatoes in the skin
and mash. Sprinkle cinnamon
powder and a handful of
walnuts.

Meal in a Bowl Dinner

Mix all together. Top with a homemade dressing.

INGREDIENTS

Shredded cabbage
Shredded carrots
Fresh cilantro
Avocados
Walnuts
Cashews
Dried cranberries

Sesame seed
Almonds
Roasted pistachios
Roasted pecans

<u>Homemade dressing:</u>
virgin olive oil and
balsamic vinegar

>>>

One Pot Chickpeas & Lentil Dinner

INGREDIENTS

1 cup cooked chickpeas
1 cup cooked lentils
1 carrot cut small lengthwise
1 small onion chopped
4 whole fresh garlic
1 small ripe tomato chopped
2 slices ginger root minced
2 tablespoons olive oil
Pinch salt to taste
¼ teaspoon allspice powder
¼ teaspoon crushed red pepper

DIRECTIONS

Heat oil on medium.

Add everything. Sauté on low heat for 15 minutes.

Eat with sliced Haas avocado.

Black-eyed Peas & Pepper Dinner

INGREDIENTS

2 cups cooked and drained black eyed peas
1/4 yellow sweet pepper chopped
2 cloves fresh garlic chopped
1 small ripe tomato chopped
1 teaspoon fresh or dried thyme leaves
¼ teaspoon Caraway seeds
2 slices beetroot cut tiny
1 small onion chopped
4 tablespoons olive oil
Pinch salt to taste
¼ teaspoon crushed red pepper

DIRECTIONS

Heat oil on medium heat. Stir in all vegetables except peas. Lower heat to low.

Cover and steam for 5 minutes stirring occasionally.

Mix in peas. Stir. Cover and simmer for 5 minutes.

Serve with a raw salad and baked potato.

>>>

Wild Salmon with Jamaican Jerk Sauce Dinner

INGREDIENTS

2 slices wild salmon rinsed with lemon juice
1 teaspoon hot jerk sauce
1/2 lemon/lime freshly squeezed juiced
Pinch of allspice powder
1 tablespoon olive oil

DIRECTIONS

Rub salmon with jerk and allspice. Pour lemon/lime juice over it. Rub on olive oil.

Heat oven to 275°. Place the baking tray in the oven and let heat for 3 minutes. Place salmon on the baking tray. Cook for about 5 minutes. Turn the oven to broil. Broil for 5 minutes.

REMEDIES

Homemade Toothpaste

The turmeric stains and is a bit messy, so take the necessary precautions to protect your surfaces and clothing.

INGREDIENTS

1 teaspoon sea salt
1 teaspoon coconut oil
1 teaspoon turmeric powder
4 drops clove oil

DIRECTIONS

Mix well. Use it as a toothpaste daily.

Ginger/Turmeric Tinctures

1 tablespoon daily can help to ward off inflammation and boost the immune system. May substitute vodka for raw, organic apple cider vinegar with the mother.

INGREDIENTS

1 pound freshly grated ginger root
1 pound freshly grated Turmeric root
Vodka or raw organic apple cider vinegar
Mason jar

DIRECTIONS

Place grated ginger and turmeric in a mason jar. Add vodka/vinegar. Place the lid tightly. Shake until well combined. Place in a dark place like the back of the cabinet. Let sit for 2 to 6 weeks.

Apple Cider Vinegar/Blackstrap Molasses/Baking Soda

I find this remedy to be very beneficial for menopausal symptoms including hot flashes, joint pain, and digestive issues like indigestion, bloating, gas, constipation. It may help to balance the pH of the blood. I take it 14 days on and 14 days off.

INGREDIENTS

¼ tsp baking soda
¼ tsp organic blackstrap molasses
1 capful organic raw apple cider vinegar with the mother

DIRECTIONS

Add ingredients to 2 ounces warm water.

Drink first thing in the morning on an empty stomach.

About the Author

Marva Riley is a Registered Nurse and author of the book *Eat Sleep Meditate a Nurse's Guide to Health.*

She advocates for a Holistic Lifestyle, which includes eating well, with a diet rich in vegetables, fruits, legumes, nuts, grains and roots, and minimizing meat and flesh.

A native of the Island of Jamaica in the West Indies, she immigrated to the US in 1989 with her two children and husband.

In her late thirties, Marva was diagnosed with a life threatening heart disease, severe depression and insomnia, bowel diseases, crippling arthritis and severe food and environment allergies. These debilitating conditions forced her to adopt a healthier way of living. After much research and the testimonials of thousands of people, Marva ate her way to her healing with a plant based diet.

Fast forward a few years and Marva now enjoys a vibrant and healthy life. She has learned how to be creative in her kitchen as she adds her favorite healthy seasonings and spices to whip up the most delicious foods.

>>

RNMarvariley.com.
info@rnmarvariley.com

www.youtube.com/channel/UCHjGAWofuawNQLPY4EomEYA
www.facebook.com/marva.riley.73